For the **Love** of
Angela

For the Love of Angela

Nancy Mayer–Whittington

Saint Catherine of Siena Press
Indianapolis

Saint Catherine of Siena Press
4812 North Park Avenue
Indianapolis, IN 46205
888-232-1492
www.saintcathpress.com
www.fortheloveofangela.com

Printed in the United States of America.

ISBN-13: 978-0-9762284-7-9
ISBN-10: 0-9762284-7-5
Library of Congress Control Number: 2007937025

Cover design and front cover photography by Mark S. Castillo. Author photograph courtesy of LifeTouch Portrait Studio of Wheaton, Maryland.

Acknowledgments may be found on page 95.

To order additional copies of this book, contact:
Theological Book Service at 877-484-1600

DEDICATION

This book is dedicated to all the children whose journey to heaven made brief their time on earth and to all the families and friends who love them. May God bless:

Francis Edward LaHood	Thomas Jones
Sara Margaret DeKemper	Christian Emmanuel Tennant
Tikvah Ariel Mellman	Yerucham Mordechai Wolf
Joseph William Folk	Andrew Michael Corcoran
Jane Susannah Levey	Eric Lyhus
Jacob Isaac Lennard	Vincent Marks Del Grosso
Kelly Marie DeCaro	Vincent Joseph Thomas
Joseph Ruppert	Matthew Anthony Thomas
Mary Ruppert	José Rodriguez
Rose Elizabeth Elderin	Audrey Neville
Emma Doreen Burns	Victoria Grace
Maura Rose Reidford	Angel Sanchez
Ezequiel Ghaffar	John Paul Rowedder
Michal Jozef Ferdock	Rose Rowedder
Michael Robert Eaton	Michael Welton
Leo Christian Stevens	Therese Welton
John Jesse Koeppels	

And to babies Mayer-Whittington, Bovello, Van Gieson, Mayer-Sangster, Stein, and to all babies named and unnamed who left the earth much too quickly.

Finally, blessings upon Matthew (Hercules) Dix and Katherine Mary Wood who though facing many challenges are joyfully still with us.

"See, I will not forget you,
I have carved you in the palm of my hand."
(cf. Isaiah 49:15-16)

FOREWORD

It is a rare privilege to enter another's soul.

For the Love of Angela is the story of Nancy Mayer-Whittington's pregnancy with Angela, her much sought-after daughter. Early in her prenatal development Angela was diagnosed with Trisomy 18, a congenital chromosomal abnormality for which there is no treatment and which inevitably results in death before or shortly after natural birth.

For the Love of Angela recounts Nancy's journey through this pregnancy, from the wonderful news of an expected sibling for her first child, Molly, and her stepdaughter, Jessica, through the birth and death of Angela. This journey is wonderfully instructive for all healthcare professionals who may deal with such life and death decisions on a daily basis, but who may sometimes lose sight of the profound effect of the diagnosis of lethal conditions on patients and their families and friends. Nancy's honesty and candor will help all who encounter anyone with this experience to become more sensitive and understanding.

We see Nancy from early on recognize the significance and value of her unborn child. We watch with admiration her efforts to provide nurturing, love, and care for her child, however long (or short) her life might be.

For the Love of Angela touches all of our humanity. On more than one occasion during my thirty years as an obstetrician/gynecologist, I would return home late at night from participating in the delivery of a child with lethal anomalies, sit at the bedside of one of our five children, and pray that I would have the spiritual strength of the mother I had just left. *For the Love of Angela* is a must read for all healthcare professionals, and indeed for all of us as we share our life journeys with each other.

Paul McCauley, MD
Silver Spring
Maryland

INTRODUCTION

I began this book to stop myself from drowning.

I thought that writing down my experience would reveal the true meaning of my daughter Angela's brief life, and I could finally come up for air. As with most things in life, however, what one has in mind at the beginning is not always what happens in the end. I thought that as I wrote I would have an epiphany—some light would go on—and I would see clearly why my infant daughter had to die, why I was chosen to carry her, and how I could incorporate her short but powerful life into my own.

Instead, the experience reveals who I was, who I am, and who I want to become. The beauty and significance of Angela are evolving revelations, not to be delivered like a thunderbolt from God, but to be appreciated and experienced like an artist preparing to unveil her masterpiece. There are rough drafts, and there are periods when creativity escapes her, but finally, she is where she is supposed to be, ready to unveil her masterpiece. I believe that Angela is a part of all that surrounds me, all that I am.

In the beginning, I wanted to understand quickly and completely all I needed to know about my daughter and her impact on me. Thankfully, we do not always get what we want. I wanted to find a way to integrate her into my life, to get past the overwhelming sadness and pain, to go on, to be happy again, and maybe even to forget. But grief, like so many other experiences, is not to be rushed through, not to be pushed aside, and not to be taken lightly. Grief, in varying stages, can last a lifetime.

I wanted to sleep through the year following Angela's death. I wanted to wake up a year from then and be well on my way to recovery. I wanted time, that wonderful healer, to step in and quickly make me better. I know now that I had to live each of those days to achieve my own perspective, my own peace with my daughter's death.

Am I at peace now, more than ten years later? Yes. Do I wish I could have achieved this peace some other way? Without a doubt. Would I give anything to have my should-have-been-thirteen-year-old daughter curled up contentedly on the couch beside me with a less enlightened, less mature, blissfully ignorant mother stroking her head? Absolutely.

My life changed forever on November 17, 1994. I have accepted that and tried to go on. Over the years, I have come to believe that Angela was a gift, an incredible four-pound, eight-ounce treasure that many people spend their lives seeking but which I was privileged to hold.

Sometimes the meaning of tragic events is revealed and we fail to recognize it. We are often too angry to do so at first, or we refuse to believe that any good can come from a tragic situation. To be honest, there is nothing good about the death of a child. It is the life you lead afterward that creates the good. It is the integration of that child's heart and soul into your being that transforms you and makes you the person you become. You can ignore this evolution, reject it, or be oblivious to it. The alternative is to accept it, reflect on it, and grow beautiful because of it. The choice is yours.

God always gives us a choice. Even when we think we have no options, we do. We can always choose our response, and for me, that response has defined my life.

As Angela was God's gift to me, this book is my gift to you.

I
- WEDNESDAY'S CHILD -

April 7, 1994, dawned strong and clear. It was a perfect spring morning, and I was feeling hopeful as I headed to work. I was on my way to a conference of my peers in court administration. I started my hour commute by praying the rosary. This rhythmic ritual clears my head, comforts me, and unites me with God. After the rosary, I went over in my mind what the day would bring. I mentally reviewed the issues we would discuss. Then, as always, my thoughts turned to my number-one priority, "When am I going to have another child?"

From my earliest recollection, I have wanted to have a big family. The fact that I did not get married until I was thirty-four did not diminish the desire. I realized that rather than the ten children I had always dreamed about, I would probably have to settle for four or five. I am the second oldest in a family of ten daughters. I wanted to replicate in my own family my wonderful childhood and great relationships with my parents, nine sisters, and growing number of brothers-in-law, nieces, and nephews.

My husband, Bryan, had been married before and had a wonderful daughter, Jessica. When we married, I became an instant and happy stepmother to six-year-old Jessica, who maintained her primary residence with her mother. A year after Bryan and I married, we had our first child, a beautiful daughter, Molly. I soon realized there was more to being a mother than just delivering a baby. I was totally, thoroughly enthralled with my infant daughter. Because Molly was more delightfully overwhelming than anything I could have dreamed of, we decided to wait a little while before attempting to have another child. The fact that I had a miscarriage at thirteen weeks with my first and only pregnancy prior to Molly seemed a distant memory, an anomaly. I knew that I was destined to have more children.

When Molly was two and a half, we decided to add to our family. At Christmas time, when I was pregnant a little more than eight weeks, we let Molly and Jessica make the joyful announcement to our family. Everyone was thrilled, and the only real problem we contemplated was the fact that our baby would arrive just in time to coincide with our annual family vacation to the beach.

A few weeks after Christmas, I started spotting. I was not too concerned at first, as I had spotted lightly with Molly. But the spotting continued, and then turned to bleeding. To be safe, I went in for an ultrasound exam. I heard the words I remembered from my first miscarriage, "I'm sorry, but there isn't anything there." When I heard those words the first time, I thought they meant that not only did I not have a baby anymore, but that I had never had a baby to begin with. I thought that somehow the baby had slipped out of me, and I had not noticed. I learned later what the doctor meant: the baby was no longer in the sac but was in the process of miscarrying.

I told Molly that our baby had been sick and had gone up to heaven. Molly did not understand. She wanted to see our baby, something I told her we could not do. She was so quiet and sad. Molly asked if we could have another baby. I assured her we could. But even as I was assuring her, I could not stop my tears. Molly climbed into my lap and hugged me. I had felt so alone after my first miscarriage. At least this time, I had Molly.

Bryan and I decided to wait a little while before trying again. When my cycle was lighter in July, I did not think much of it. When I began in early August to experience some of the signs of pregnancy, I took an at-home pregnancy test. It was positive. Within a day or two I started spotting. All I could think was, Not again. My third miscarriage? *I called my doctor, and he scheduled an ultrasound. The internal ultrasound showed a sac, but the size of the sac did not comport with my cycle dates. Although I was beginning to bleed more heavily, the doctor advised against a D & C on the off-chance that I still had a viable pregnancy. I, too, wanted to do anything I could to preserve the pregnancy. I was beginning to think that what so many women did so effortlessly would be impossible for me to repeat. Over the next two weeks I bled heavily and eventually passed the tissue that had been my baby's life. The following week I was at the beach for my family's yearly vacation and could only think that if all had gone well with my fourth pregnancy, I would have been at home caring for my new baby. The fact that I had suffered a third miscarriage so recently only added to the pain.*

When I returned from our family vacation to the beach, I made an appointment with my doctor to discuss my options. I was advised that most doctors do not actively pursue answers to miscarriage problems until a woman has had at least three miscarriages. I now qualified for this unlucky status, but my doctor said that since I had had a successful pregnancy between the first and second miscarriages, I should wait until a third consecutive miscarriage. Even as he said the words, I knew he did not want to see me go through this again. He recommended that we do a few preliminary tests to determine my proges-

terone level. Those tests did not reveal anything out of the ordinary, and so I went to an infertility specialist for further testing. The infertility doctor recommended that my husband and I go through some preliminary genetics testing to see if we were chromosomally compatible. The doctor warned that the tests were rather expensive and may not reveal the cause of our problem, but at least they could rule out some things. My husband and I agreed to undergo the tests. The results revealed nothing about why I had experienced three miscarriages. The doctor told me that even if we were to pursue more testing, all the known tests for determining the causes of a miscarriage could only account for 50 percent of the miscarriages. In other words, 50 percent of the causes of a miscarriage remain unknown to this day. He told us that even after having suffered three miscarriages, I still had an 87 percent chance of carrying a baby to term.

Bryan and I decided to forego any additional testing. Instead, we opted to try a progesterone supplement with my next pregnancy. Although an earlier test had not indicated a problem with my progesterone level, my doctor thought it might be worthwhile to take the supplement. In late January, I realized my cycle was two weeks late. On my forty-first birthday, February 2, 1994, I tried an at-home pregnancy test, and it was positive. I called my doctor, who immediately ordered the progesterone prescription for me. I could only get the prescription at a pharmacy near my doctor's office. Because it would not be ready until late in the day, I left my office in plenty of time to arrive at the pharmacy before it closed. Unfortunately, an accident tied up traffic, so I arrived too late. The pharmacy was closed. That night I began spotting. The next day the bleeding continued, and I gave up on getting the prescription and resigned myself to a fourth miscarriage.

Two months after my fourth miscarriage, I arrived at my court administration conference and went about the day attending meetings and visiting with colleagues. At one point, I was called to the director's office, where I found out that I had been selected to be one of four nationwide recipients of the Director's Award for Outstanding Leadership. When I returned to my office that day, I called my husband and told him the good news. We made plans to go out to dinner. Unfortunately, I was unable to leave the office on time to keep our reservation. Instead, Bryan picked up carry-out, and we had a nice dinner with Molly who, at age four, did not understand what we were celebrating. After dinner, we went upstairs to get ready for bed. As I was getting ready, I remembered that I had purchased a home-pregnancy kit a few days earlier. I counted up the days and realized I was only a week late. I decided to take the test anyway. Maybe the fact that I had won the award earlier in the day was a good sign.

The test was positive. With cautious optimism, I told Bryan. He hugged me and said, "Maybe this is it. Let's hope so." Although outwardly I tried to appear positive, inwardly I was holding my breath and praying. Prayer was my constant recourse, my steady companion.

II
- HOPE SPRINGS ETERNAL -

The next day I called my doctor and told him the good news. He ordered a progesterone prescription and told me to begin taking it that afternoon. Because the progesterone components must be mixed immediately before the prescription is dispensed, only a few pharmacies in our area could prepare it. It took awhile to find a pharmacy that had the progesterone on hand, but we finally located one. I began the required dose that evening. For the next few days I kept "the blood vigil." Every few minutes, I would check for bleeding. When a week went by without any sign of blood, I began to relax. I had my first doctor's appointment scheduled for April 22. At my urging, the receptionist, who knew me and my history well, agreed to put off my first appointment for as long as possible, as I had begun to perceive that appointments early in pregnancy jinxed the life of my baby. Although I am not really superstitious, neither am I the most optimistic person.

When the day of my doctor's appointment arrived, I was so happy because I had not spotted at all, and other than feeling sick all the time, I did not have any indication of a problem with my pregnancy. During the examination, however, my doctor seemed to hesitate a little. He asked how far along I was, and I told him I was about six weeks pregnant. Frowning, he felt my stomach. When I asked what was wrong, he said that my uterus did not feel exactly as it should after six weeks. Acknowledging that my tilted uterus made it difficult to get a good reading at this point in the pregnancy, my doctor said it would probably be a good idea to get a blood sample for a quantitative pregnancy test, a test that would give him specific information about the gestational age of the baby. He took the sample and said he would have the results on Monday.

When I left his office, I was depressed. Since I was over six weeks pregnant and had not experienced any bleeding, I had started to believe that everything would finally work out. Now the doctor was saying that the pregnancy did not feel quite right. I was so upset that I did not go back to work but instead went directly to a fast-food restaurant for a bacon cheeseburger, French fries, and large Coke. I had never had a craving for fast food, so I rarely ate it. But that day I felt like I needed some comfort food.

My doctor had told me that I should call his office at approximately

15

10:30 Monday morning for the lab results. I watched the clock anxiously for two hours, and then, when 10:30 struck, I was suddenly afraid. Although I said a quick prayer and reminded myself that I would survive even if the pregnancy did not, I could not bring myself to dial the number right away. I just sat at my desk and thought about how much I wanted this baby. I bargained with God, saying, "If you just let me have this baby, I won't ask for another thing." The song "Sometimes I Thank God for Unanswered Prayers" played over and over again in my head. *If the doctor's news proved not to be the answer to my prayers, would there be a silver lining? Would I be all right?* I got up from my desk and went into the bathroom. I just stood there looking into the mirror. Finally, I decided to make the call.

I went back to my desk, picked up the receiver, and dialed. The receptionist answered and said she would put one of the doctors on the phone. My doctor's partner picked up the extension and said the sweetest words I had heard in a long time, "Everything looks good!" He said that my blood count was comparable to being right in the middle of my first trimester, and that that would comport with the dates of my last cycle. He went on to say that I could have an ultrasound to confirm the length of my pregnancy. Without hesitation I agreed. With my history, I needed the visual confirmation of a healthy baby. We settled on a 1:00 appointment for that afternoon.

I immediately called Bryan to see if he could go with me. Poor Bryan had never been present at a good ultrasound reading. He had accompanied me both times when we had heard those fateful words, "I'm sorry, but there's nothing there." My parents had been with me for the one good ultrasound that I had received during Molly's pregnancy, as Bryan could not get time off from work.

This time Bryan was able to attend. Together we sat in the clinic waiting room, my anxiety mounting. My heart was beating so fast, like a drum pounding in my head. I tried to read a magazine, but I was so wrapped up in my fears that I could not concentrate on anything else. Finally, I resorted to counting the ceiling tiles and then the little dots in each tile. By looking up, I could avoid eye contact with the other women around me. I was sure they were having blissfully uneventful pregnancies. To add insult to injury, I had gotten sick right after we arrived at the clinic.

When I was finally called back, I did not have enough fluid in my bladder to get a good image of the baby; the technician was forced to try an alternative, an internal ultrasound. The first thing I heard was the heartbeat.

I wanted to get down on my knees and thank God for that sound. I was so happy I started to cry. Seeing my tears, the technician thought she was hurting me, but I told her I was just so relieved to hear a heartbeat after four miscarriages. She showed us our baby's head, spine, and the beginning of arms and legs. They were the most beautiful pictures I had ever seen. Bryan stood beside me, holding my hand and commenting on the wonders of technology. Considering that our baby was only one inch long, the clarity and detail of the pictures were incredible.

A doctor at the clinic confirmed the technician's observations and told me that everything looked fine. She knew of my history of miscarriages, and while a first trimester spontaneous abortion was still a possibility, she gave me good odds that this baby was a keeper. The technician printed out two pictures for us to take home. She printed "Hi Mom" on one picture and "Hi Dad" on the other. I left the building feeling like I was walking on air. It reminded me of the way I had felt when they confirmed my pregnancy with Molly. Right at that time, I did not have a care in the world. This was in sharp contrast from the times we had gone to the clinic just to confirm what we already suspected, that our baby was gone.

Bryan went back to work, and I went to my parents' house to show them the ultrasound pictures of their newest grandchild. They were suitably impressed and thankful that our prayers had been answered.

The next two weeks floated by. Then, to my disbelief, I began to spot one Saturday morning. I immediately laid down and proceeded to stay as quiet as I could. I was afraid of losing the baby but even more afraid that I really had no control over the situation. Taking to bed before the other miscarriages had not changed the outcome, so I read a lot and prayed even more. I read *Lives of the Saints,* searching for inspiration and guidance in the hardships the saints had endured. I begged God to bless me with the courage I needed as I read *Chicken Soup for the Mother's Soul.*

I just kept asking God to let me keep this baby.

By Monday morning I was a nervous wreck. I called my doctor right away. He asked if I was bleeding extensively, and I told him about the spotting. He said it was probably nothing to worry about, but if I wanted to have it checked out, he would schedule another ultrasound reading. Not having many positive thoughts, I really needed the reassurance of an ultrasound. My doctor set an appointment for that afternoon, explaining that I would see one of his associates.

Again, Bryan went with me. The wait seemed endless. I memorized the pattern of the carpet and counted and recounted the number of ceiling tiles. I could not concentrate on reading or even on talking to Bryan. I just wanted to find out if my baby was all right. When the technician called my name, I was shaking so hard I could not keep my knees still. The first thing that came on the screen was that wonderfully reassuring, beautifully beating heart. I relaxed a little as the technician took several pictures.

When the doctor came into the room, she quickly brought me down to earth: "There seems to be a problem with the baby. I don't want to alarm you too much, but I think the area around the back of the baby's head is a little thicker than it should be." I asked her what that meant, and she said it could be nothing. She said it was a pivotal time in the baby's development and entirely possible that the area would resolve itself in three or four weeks. She told me I should have another ultrasound at that time. Bryan and I left the clinic not knowing what to think.

The next few weeks passed uneventfully. The spotting seemed to stop. I did not experience any more outward signs of problems with my pregnancy. Inwardly, I was a basket case, but I tried to reassure myself that everything would be all right. I kept telling myself that God would not let me get this far only to learn that our baby had serious problems. At my next monthly doctor's appointment, I was reassured that everything looked good and that the information I had received at the ultrasound appointment was probably just a red herring. I began to feel a little more confident and actually bought some new maternity clothes—not that I needed any. With my nine sisters, many of whom had been pregnant, we had quite a collection. However, given my need to do something positive, the mere act of buying maternity clothes served to confirm the existence of this new baby I was carrying.

III
- SHOCK AND DISBELIEF -

In my twelfth week of pregnancy, I went back for a repeat of the ultrasound. The technician took a number of pictures and then left the room without saying much to Bryan and me. When the doctor came in, she told us that she had good news and bad news. The good news was that the thickening in the back of the head appeared to have cleared up. The bad news was that she had spotted some other problems. Our baby had a diaphragmatic hernia, which meant that the stomach was protruding into the chest cavity, and a clubfoot. Both conditions, we were told, could be corrected by surgery, which would more than likely have to take place right after our baby was born. The doctor told me it was not as devastating as it sounded, that they could do wonderful things these days, but nothing could stop the tears from running down my face. I just sat there, holding Bryan's hand, trying to make sense of it all.

Why me? Why this? Didn't we deserve a healthy baby? Hadn't we paid our dues with four miscarriages? When was this nightmare going to end? When would our life be "happily ever after"?

Bryan and I barely spoke on the ride home from the ultrasound appointment. Both of us were engrossed in our own thoughts. When I tried to talk to Bryan, all he could say was "Don't worry. I'm sure it will be all right." Later, after we had put Molly to bed, I learned more about Bryan's reaction. He did not fully believe the doctor. He had been uncomfortable with her after our last visit, primarily because of her bedside manner. She had displayed no empathy for us in our circumstances, hurriedly rattling off the list of problems our baby faced, conveying the impression that what mattered the most to her was her next appointment. When it turned out that she had been wrong about the thickening in the back of the baby's head, Bryan assumed her second diagnosis was mistaken as well.

I tried to tell him that it was not a good idea to count on her being wrong. I did not want to believe her either, but she had been quite specific about what the monitor was showing her. Bryan said he could not make out anything on the monitor and did not see how she could either. I tried to tell him that reading the monitor was her job, that she was probably much better at it than we were, but he would not budge. I let him go to sleep with his defense mechanisms firmly in place, and, not for the first time, I felt very alone. I sat in our sunroom and cried. I was worried and scared, but even more, I was hurt. Bryan seemed to be able to wall himself off from our baby's problems and go to sleep while I was left alone with only my thoughts as company. Each miscarriage had left me feeling the same way: Bryan on the outside looking in and me on the inside holding on, alone. He came in and out of the pregnancy almost at will, while I stayed attached to the baby and then to the memory, forever.

I spoke with my doctor the next day, and he echoed the diagnosis of the doctor at the ultrasound clinic. The baby's problems were correctable, and everything else looked good. I had had my blood drawn earlier that week for a three-part screening test. Once we had those results, we would know more about our baby's condition.

Each morning before I went to work I would take out a card my sister Cecilia had given to me. Cecilia's faith in God and in prayer was a constant source of inspiration for me. The card had a simple prayer on it: "You can't. He can. Let him." It was easy to pray these words, but so difficult to let God take over. I could control so little of the situation, whether it was diet, exercise, or anything else I thought would influence my baby's life. Prayer was the only consolation I had.

A week later, just as I was going to conduct my morning staff meeting, my doctor called. He had the results of my "triple screen" blood test, and he sounded distressed. This particular test measured three substances in the blood: alpha-fetoprotein, chorionic gonadotropin, and estriol. The results can suggest the presence of spinal bifida or other chromosomal abnormality. My result showed that the baby was at risk for one such abnormality, Trisomy 18. I had never heard of it.

Our doctor explained that in a normal conception, the mother and father each contribute 23 chromosomes to conceive a baby with 46 chromosomes in each cell, one pair of each type of chromosome. Trisomy 18 most commonly occurs when a pair of #18 chromosomes from the mother or the father fails to separate and thus remains in one egg or one sperm cell. Thus, rather than a pair of #18 chromosomes, the baby receives three copies of #18 chromosome—the condition known as trisomy.

When I asked him how Trisomy 18 would affect the baby, he likened it to Down's syndrome with much more severe consequences. He called the condition "incompatible with life." He went on to say that in most cases the baby dies *in utero*, and the rare baby that survives generally has to be institutionalized due to the amount of care the person requires. "Incompatible with life...die *in utero*...institutionalized..." I could not take it all in. I was numb and could barely hear the doctor say that an amniocentesis ("amnio") could still rule out this condition. The "triple screen" test, after all, did have a certain probability of error. After telling him to schedule the amniocentesis, I asked him one last agonizing question. I asked him if a diaphragmatic hernia and clubfoot were consistent with a Trisomy 18 diagnosis. Very quietly, he said yes.

I slowly put the phone down. I did not know what to do next. In the conference room next door there were ten people waiting for me to conduct my weekly senior staff meeting. If I went into the bathroom I would start crying, and I knew the tears would not stop. I asked God to help me. I willed myself to go into the next room and begin the meeting. It was the first of many times I would have to act like everything was fine when my heart was breaking and my whole world was turning upside down. When it was over, I wanted to go into my office, get my stuff, and head home. In order to get through the meeting, I had promised myself I would leave the minute it concluded. During the meeting, however, a colleague reminded me that I had to speak at a retirement ceremony that evening for four of our senior employees. It would be a formal occasion at a nearby restaurant, an event which the news from my doctor had completely erased from my mind.

After the meeting, I went back to my office and closed my door. I sat on my couch and asked God what I should do. By this time the tears were streaming down my face, and I was shaking uncontrollably.

How could this be happening to me? How could my baby, this baby that I wanted so much, have so many problems? How could it have a chromosomal condition when our tests had ruled out chromosomal incompatibilities? What was I going to do? How could I go on?

After what seemed like forever, I felt Bryan saying to me, "We'll get through this, one day at a time, one hour at a time." I had not had a chance to talk to him because he was out of the office that day, and I would not be able to reach him until evening. He knew I had to attend the retirement dinner and would not be home until later. If I reached him before the ceremony, he would tell me that the people would understand if I did not want to go through with it. But I also knew at this point that I did not want to share this news with anyone but my family. I needed time to digest it without a lot of advice from others.

As I sat crying in my office, I prayed for guidance. When my tears stopped falling, I lifted my head and looked around my office, searching for something that would inspire me, or at least distract me. I went over to my credenza and picked up the latest picture of Molly and Jessica, my two healthy, happy children. I tried to tell myself how lucky I was to have them. My attempts to focus on something positive were interrupted by a phone call from my sister Kathleen. I was determined not to say anything, but, as soon as she asked how I was doing, I broke down. I told her about my conversation with the doctor, and that I was not going to say anything about it to my family and friends until the amniocentesis had confirmed or ruled out the diagnosis. Kathleen was a model of support and understanding, and while she left it to me to decide on my course of action, she also pointed out that she was a big believer in the power of prayer. She thought that if I shared the news with my family, all of their prayers would be joined with mine for the safety and health of my baby. I agreed to think about it and, of course, to talk to Bryan.

The rest of the day passed in a haze of work activities and endless thoughts about my baby's life. I tried to concentrate on the impending ceremony. I reminded myself that the four soon-to-be-retired employees were counting on me to send them off to their retirement years in grand fashion. I could not be selfish and think about myself.

That night I had to endure so many well-meaning, thoughtful people who congratulated me on my pregnancy. A number of our retired employees had returned for the ceremony, and it was the first time they had seen me in my obviously pregnant state. They were so happy for me and Bryan, and I remember thinking, *How can I tell them my baby might die?* I accepted their congratulations and kept quiet about everything else.

Finally it was over, and I could leave. Before I could reach my car, the tears started. There was no reason to hold back. The retirement dinner was over. I could retreat to my private world again. I sat in my car and cried.

Molly was in bed when I arrived home, and Bryan was sprawled out on the couch watching television. I stopped for a moment and looked at him. He looked so relaxed, so content. It was all about to change. For a moment I thought about going up to bed and pretending this was all a bad dream. I said a prayer, took a deep breath, and went into the room. Greeting each other, I told him the ceremony was fine and my speeches had gone well. Then the tears came. He thought I had had an accident or that something had happened at dinner. When I finally told him, between sobs, about the conversation with my doctor, he wrapped me in his arms and assured me the amniocentesis would rule out Trisomy 18. He said that God would not do this to us after all we had been through. I told him that I did not think God worked in that way. I was not sure exactly how God worked, to be honest, but I knew that bad things happen to good people. We did not get an automatic pass.

IV
- FEAR AND WAITING -

The next few weeks were agonizing. I cannot describe how painful my life was or how slowly the time passed. Though trivial compared to what our baby was facing, every problem at work, at home, or with traffic seemed magnified a dozen times. I had a recurrent dream in which the doctor came to me with good news and bad news. The good news was the baby did not have Trisomy 18 and, in fact, was perfect. The bad news was the amnio had caused a miscarriage (as it can 1 percent of the time), and our baby was gone. These thoughts haunted me every day.

A few days before the scheduled amnio, I felt our baby move for the first time. That little movement jolted me out of my despair. Just for a moment, I had a taste of pure joy. Despite all we were facing, our baby was still alive. There was still hope, and, to me, our baby was more real than ever.

Bryan accompanied me to the amnio, which was fairly easy, and then I went back to work. My doctor had told me it could take up to ten days to get the results. He said that if everything was fine, the center that had conducted the amnio would call me. If the results were not good, he would be the one to deliver the news. And so we waited.

Six days later, at the end of my workday, my doctor called. Since I thought it was too early to have the amnio results, I was ill prepared for what followed. His first words made my heart stop: "Well, I guess you know that since I am calling, the news is not good." He went on to say that the test had confirmed that our baby did indeed have Trisomy 18, and he was truly sorry to have to give me this news. Somehow I thanked him for calling and hung up the phone. I picked up my purse, told my secretary that I had just received bad news, and went to my car.

The tears started falling when I climbed behind the wheel. I honestly do not remember driving home. I was in another world, shocked by the final confirmation. In a daze, I kept thinking, *My baby is sick. My baby is going to die. How would I ever survive this? How would I go on?* I went through a range of emotions on the drive home, from despair to fear and then to anger. I was angry with myself for having had some hope. *Why did I let myself think everything might be all right? Why had I not just spent the past few weeks preparing for the inevitable? What did I expect after all the early signs? Why had I not better pre-*

pared myself? And I was so very mad at God. *I had trusted Him to take care of my baby and He had failed me. How could I ever trust Him again?* Then the fear returned and I did not know what to do.

Bryan and I arrived home at the same time. One look at my face and he knew. We stumbled inside and collapsed into each other's arms. We held on and cried together. My aunt, who had been watching Molly, hugged me and cried with us. She tried to think of something to say to console us, but it was impossible. She said God would help us through this, to which I thought, almost against my will, *Why was God putting us through this?* But I did not want to get through this. I wanted it to go away. I wanted my baby to live.

Shortly after my aunt left, my parents arrived. Tipped off by my aunt, they were at a loss for words. I remember holding on to my mother and willing her to make it all better. But she could not, and I knew it. When we composed ourselves, my mother asked about the reliability of the amnio results. I told her the results were 99.9 percent accurate. My mother then asked about Trisomy 18, but we did not have any answers except the limited information our doctor had provided several weeks ago. I really knew next to nothing about this condition that would kill our baby.

V

- Our Little Baby Doll -

After a sleepless night, Bryan and I decided to take the day off from our jobs and organize our thoughts. The fog that had come over us after confirmation of our baby's condition was lifting a little. I felt my numbness give way to rational thought and many questions. Having regained some of my composure now that my tears were utterly spent, I called my doctor. He gave me the name of the doctor who chaired the Department of Genetics and Metabolism at Children's National Medical Center in Washington, D.C. The hospital was less than an hour away, and fortunately my doctor was able to schedule an appointment for us that afternoon. Before I could begin to prepare myself for what that appointment might bring, I asked my doctor if I was carrying a boy or a girl. He did not know, but the technician who had conducted my amnio did.

I was not sure right away if I wanted to call the technician. So much of this pregnancy had been defined by telephone calls. The first call had brought euphoric confirmation. I was really pregnant! The second call had brought shock and disbelief with the news that my baby may have a life-threatening condition. With the third call had come despair in the confirmation that our baby would most likely die. *Could I make one more phone call? Did I really want to know if I was carrying a boy or a girl? The second daughter who will never wear Molly's hand-me-downs or the first son we will never know? Would one answer make it better? Would either answer make it worse?*

I felt frozen in my confusion. The fog was returning, seeping slowly, relentlessly. I stood up and shook my head, trying to untangle my thoughts. I dialed the number and waited while the technician fetched my report. A few minutes later she returned and said, "You have a little girl." *A little girl, a little sister, my second daughter, my baby who will never grow up.* I do not remember hanging up. I sat for what seemed like hours while the news sank in. *Now our baby is a "she," not an "it." Would she have dark hair like Molly or blond hair like Jessica? What would she look like?* I left our bedroom and went to find Bryan. I tried to speak, but the words would not come out. The tears which I thought were dried up came rushing back. Finally I said, "We have a little girl." Bryan put his head in his hands and rocked back and forth. Then he looked up at me and whispered, "Our little baby doll."

Bryan and I drove to Children's National Medical Center in silence.

After two hours of talking with the specialist, the tiny thread of hope floating in my heart was gone. He concluded the consultation by saying, "Let me tell you what I think your choices are in this situation. You can let your daughter die peacefully in your arms surrounded by people who love her or you can let her die in an operating room surrounded by strangers." Those words, administered softly with dignity and care, framed the entire visit. Those words put the whole situation into the perspective of my daughter's feelings, my daughter's life.

The doctor with whom we were meeting had delivered or participated in the births of more than two hundred babies with Trisomy 18. He said that the condition occurs approximately once every three thousand live births. The life expectancy for girls is approximately thirty days; for boys, twenty. With great comfort and empathy, the doctor went over the problems associated with Trisomy 18, such as the club (twisted) feet or legs and clenched fists. Also common is a diaphragmatic hernia that causes the heart to impinge upon one of the lungs and the stomach impinge upon the other lung. As a consequence, the lungs fail to develop properly and the baby enters the world unable to breathe independently. In many cases, the heart fails to develop as it should. Unlike Trisomy 21 or Down's syndrome, the risk of having a baby with Trisomy 18 does not increase dramatically with the age of the mother. Strangely, that made me feel a little better, knowing my age was not the only factor.

The doctor went on to paint an even grimmer picture of our baby's development—severe mental retardation, growth deficiency, cardiopulmonary disorders, and the potential for many other abnormalities. In addition, this constellation of disorders would make it difficult if not impossible to withstand anesthesia. In all likelihood, any surgical effort to help our baby would unwittingly cause her death.

As the doctor spoke, my mind wandered to hopes of heart transplants, lung transplants, embryonic surgeries, and other life-saving operations that I had read about but of which I had no firsthand knowledge. Unfortunately, our baby was not a candidate for any of these remedies because of the extremely poor condition of so many of her vital organs. We listened patiently but with increasing hopelessness. At no time were we directed to a single, specific outcome. The doctor assured us that the hospital was there to help Bryan and me decide what we wanted to do and would support us both emotionally and with all their resources no matter what our decision.

Even though the doctor did not push us in any one direction, we essentially had three options. We could abort the baby at this early stage of her development, knowing that 80 to 90 percent of babies with Trisomy 18 do not progress to a live birth. Second, we could continue the pregnancy and take dramatic steps to prolong our daughter's life with respirators and surgery, knowing that she was a poor candidate for any invasive procedure. Finally, we could continue the pregnancy and take no dramatic steps to prolong her life.

The doctor gave us a stack of reading material on Trisomy 18 and how other couples had dealt with the condition in their infants. By the time we left the office, my usual clarity had vanished. The fog was once again enveloping me. The experience was more like a bad dream than reality. I wanted to wake up and find that my baby was healthy, but the papers in my hands and the doctor's discussion were too real to be a dream.

On the ride home, Bryan and I discussed our soon-to-be five-year-old daughter, Molly. I could not hold back my tears as we talked about how much she was looking forward to this baby and how terrific a big sister she would have made. Before we had left for the hospital, we told Molly our baby was very sick and might even die. Molly ran from the room crying, and only Bryan was able to talk to her. I had just sat there too overwhelmed with my own emotions to help Molly with hers.

At that moment, I was glad Bryan and I reacted to things differently. I had fallen apart at the news and Bryan had been more stoic. Bryan was able to be there for Molly when I could not. The different ways we reacted to the many challenges we encountered with the pregnancy were often a source of friction, but it was better that one of us could keep the other going. It would have been disastrous if both of us fell apart at the same time.

We had specifically talked with the doctor and his assistant at Children's National Medical Center about Molly and what to tell her about her sister's condition. He advised us, given her age and maturity, to be open and honest with her. They told us to tell her that her sister had something called Trisomy 18, and that because of this she would have a difficult time trying to live. The doctor said not to tell her our baby was sick. In the future, Molly would get sick and might associate that with her sister's inability to live. My heart sank when I realized our mistake in telling her, but the reality was that we had to prepare Molly for the probable outcome of her sister's death. I thought, *How do I do this? How do I prepare Molly for her sister's death when I am not prepared myself?* He gave us an article outlining how one couple had dealt with their five-year-old's reaction to his baby sister's death. The article was touching, but heartbreaking.

The author told of the experience of a couple whose second child was stillborn. Their five-year-old son Josh had accompanied them to be hospital, for they had not anticipated any problems. After the shock of learning that their just-delivered daughter was not alive, they struggled with what to tell Josh. They decided to bring him into the room to see his little sister and take their cues from him.

Josh accepted the news from his parents that his sister had died and would soon be in heaven. He asked his parents if her name was still Agnes, the name that they had picked out together as a family. Josh began to speak to Agnes and told her that she wouldn't be alone in heaven. He explained that his pet frog, Petey, had died a few months ago and that Petey would be there to keep her company. Josh had shown his parents a remarkable ability to accept the news of his sister's death and to relate it to the only connection that he had with death. This reaction gave his parents some small measure of comfort in a tragic situation.

I almost could not finish the remaining articles, though one newsletter did encourage us somewhat. There seemed to be several children with the condition who had not only survived the pregnancy but had celebrated a first and, in two cases, a second birthday. But then the words of the doctor at Children's National Medical Center came back to us. This particular newsletter, he had told us, took into account all Trisomy 18 births in the U.S. and Canada. While the success stories were causes for optimism, we needed to be realistic too. Of the two hundred live births the doctor had witnessed, only two children were still alive. One was two years old; the other, six. In the latter case, the doctors were not quite sure if he truly had Trisomy 18.

After several days of reading, I put the articles down. I felt like I could not read one more article about a baby dying. For one thing, they were all written from a perspective I did not share, that of one who had survived the tragedy and been able to continue living after years of support and care. Also, all the articles were about families dealing with the unexpected death of a child shortly after birth. None of the articles dealt with families who knew well before the pregnancy came to term that their baby would most likely die. I vowed that if I survived this time in my life with my senses still intact, I would write a book for anyone who came after me in this situation.

After much soul searching, prayer, discussion, and tears, Bryan and I decided to do what I had privately known all along. Even from the first minute, when I began to suspect our baby might have serious problems, I knew we were going to continue the pregnancy. We were going to give our baby as many chances as we could. We ultimately felt that our baby's life was in God's hands, not ours.

We also decided to name our unborn daughter. So many of the articles suggested that this was a way to give the baby an identity and a measure of dignity. We settled on *Angela*. My mother said we should start thinking about her as our own special angel, and thus the name Angela fit perfectly. Some parents resist thinking about their babies as angels, arguing that it depersonalizes the situation and plays down all the sadness and grief involved. But I found comfort in my mother's words; it helped to make me think that my Angela, who probably would not survive this pregnancy, would live on in heaven. The name gave her the only life I could imagine.

It may sound odd to some, but for me the toughest decision was not whether to continue the pregnancy. My Catholic faith and the example my parents had set for me by living that faith every day, in good times and in bad, made that decision virtually automatic. The tough decision was what to do if Angela, with her poor prognosis, survived to a live birth. Bryan and I both concluded that a life of machines and institutions was not for our daughter. If Angela made it into this world alive, we would not force her to undergo a fruitless operation in an attempt of put off the inevitable. We would hold her and hug her and love her, but we would not give her over to a surgeon and expect him or her to work a miracle. If Angela lived longer than a few minutes we would make her comfortable for as long as she lived. This was by no means our final decision; there were still more tests to be done.

The next several months were the hardest of my life. Every night I would go to sleep asking God for a miracle. Every morning I would wake up and realize that nothing had changed. I persuaded myself to fall asleep clinging to the dream of waking up from this nightmare. The next morning, the grim reality of Angela's condition was like a weight forcing me to stay in bed. The daily struggles left me exhausted.

A few days after we received confirmation of the Trisomy 18 diagnosis, I spoke to my doctor about continuing the pregnancy. He reassured me that he supported my decision. Because I had a high-risk pregnancy, he asked me to see him every two weeks. At each meeting he listened for the baby's heartbeat, and each time it came through loud and clear. Often, babies with Trisomy 18 have cardiac malformations. We knew from one of the ultrasound images that Angela's heart had only two chambers, in contrast to the four chambers found in a normal heart. Despite having a a damaged heart, Angela's heartbeat was so strong and steady that the doctor commented on it regularly. He said that if he hadn't known of Angela's condition, he would never have suspected the presence of Trisomy 18. Nevertheless, there was still a good chance that Angela would die *in utero*.

For the first month or two, I prayed that God would take Angela early. I wanted God to end my pregnancy so I would not have to make a decision about artificially prolonging Angela's life. *Maybe if I did not carry her to term, maybe I would not have as much time to bond with her. Maybe it would be easier on me. Maybe my recovery would be faster.*

But then, as the months passed, and Angela grew, moved regularly, and began to kick me, my prayers changed. I started to pray that I would get the chance to see her, hold her, and hug her. After four miscarriages and endless questions about each baby's character and personality, I wanted to see Angela. Even if she was not going to live long or even at all, I just wanted to see her. That wish grew stronger with each passing day.

At my first appointment after Angela's Trisomy 18 condition was confirmed, I learned something surprising. My doctor asked me if, when the time was appropriate, I wanted to induce labor so I could have some control over the date of Angela's birth. I thought about this for a moment and asked him what other women in my situation had decided. He replied, "I've never had a woman continue her pregnancy. All of my patients, when faced with a life-threatening diagnosis, have chosen to terminate the pregnancy." I was stunned into silence. I did not think my desire to continue my pregnancy was that unusual. My doctor interrupted my thoughts and quietly reassured me: "This is your first time and my first time, so we will learn together."

VI
- Letting Go and Letting God -

Every time someone congratulated me about my pregnancy, I was confronted with an enormous dilemma. Should I tell them the truth or keep quiet? Ironically, I did not want to spoil their happiness by telling them about Angela's likely death. These conversations were achingly difficult, for they made me relive my story over and over again.

I finally decided that certain conditions had to be met in order for me to speak candidly about Angela. If the congratulations came from a total stranger, I said nothing and accepted their best wishes. If it was a person I knew only slightly and perhaps would not see again soon, I said nothing and let him or her enjoy my pregnancy. Of course, I told my family and some close friends the truth, and gradually word spread at my office. Because I work in a large building and see a variety of people each day, it became difficult to keep straight who knew and who did not.

Breaking the news to people was practically a trauma in itself. They were so shocked and unprepared, and many could not hold back tears. They had no idea what to say to me and just nodded wordlessly as I tried to comfort them. At a time when I was in dire need of consolation, despite having had time to adjust to Angela's condition, I frequently found myself placed in the position of consoling other people. It was like living in two different worlds: my Angela world, which was my name for the private purgatory I inhabited daily, and the world of my family, friends, and work. In my Angela world, I was lonely and scared. In my public world, I acted as if I were resigned to the inevitable.

In an effort to keep my perspective and sanity during this time, I kept a journal. The following entry reads like so many others:

Yesterday was not a good day. I felt like I was on the verge of tears all day. I don't know why I get so emotional all the time. Okay, okay, so I guess I do know why, but it still surprises me that the tears come so easily. I cry at Mass, in the car, in the shower, at my office, at dinner, you name a place and I've cried there. When my sister Eileen asked me about Angela, I thought I was doing really well. I was telling her some things, and then, I just started crying. I told Eileen I was sorry, I was getting better about not crying all the time, but sometimes, it is just so hard. Eileen said she didn't know how I was doing it. She said she thought I was incredibly strong and not to worry about cry-

ing. I really appreciated that because I want to talk to my sisters about Angela. I want to tell them a little of what we are going through and what we have decided. But, I get so mad that I can't talk without crying. I'm afraid they are not going to ask because they are afraid it will upset me. And, yes, it does upset me, but I still need to talk about it. Anyway, I hope I didn't blow it yesterday. I hope my sisters, my family, and everyone still ask me about Angela.

Besides capturing my thoughts in words, I also realized that I needed to think about documenting as much of Angela's brief life as I could. The solution was to take pictures—lots of them. I also knew I wanted to have a backup camera in case something happened to the first camera. I also had a Polaroid camera to take so I would have some instantly developed pictures to hold onto after they took Angela away.

In so many of the articles I had read, the thing that parents most regretted in the wake of their infants' death was the lack of photographs of their child. If they had not taken pictures, they would have. If they had taken a few shots, they would have taken more. Many of the mothers in the articles had endured the death of their baby at a time when hospitals responded to their losses rather insensitively. Many hospitals did not realize the importance of simply letting the family hold their infant, even after he or she has died. In some cases, the babies had literally been swept away, and the mothers never saw them again.

I decided that I would not let this happen to me. I had no idea how much time I would be able to spend with my daughter, even after her death, but my plan was to take as many pictures as could be taken and to be with her until the last possible moment. Having a plan made me feel some measure of control in a situation that was mostly out of my control. I was haunted by one thought in particular. I was afraid that once I had been given my daughter I would not be able to give her back. I had dreams of sneaking her out of the hospital and taking her home with me. I had no idea what I would do with her once I was home, but the feeling was overwhelming. It was not a rational thought. It was more the thought of a desperate mother somehow trying to prolong the inevitable, trying to hold on a little longer. I was so afraid I would lose control, that I would go over the edge and not come back. I was afraid the reality of Angela's death would be so unbearable that I would lose my grip and slip over the edge of sanity.

I tried to do what I usually do when I have trouble dealing with a situation. I tried to think my way out, to think my way through it. I tried to go through in my mind what was going to happen so I could prepare myself mentally, spiritually, and emotionally. I tried to imagine what it would be like to give birth to a child and then watch the child die. I finally realized that I could not find a way to walk myself through the inevitable and predict how I would react. Instead of trying to imagine the unimaginable in the hope of somehow exerting control over it, I turned to my journal:

> *I know I am trying to approach this situation much like I would approach any other tough situation in my life. I'm trying to think it through. I'm trying to prepare myself for every possible outcome: Angela is stillborn; Angela dies right after she is born; Angela lives a few hours; and on and on. But, I feel like I can't do it. I can't project today's feeling on a time in the future. I thought by planning in my mind for every possible outcome, I would better prepare myself emotionally and mentally for the birth. But that is not possible. No matter how hard I want to ease the pain of what will happen, I cannot. I am going to have to live the pain when it happens. I am trying to retain as much control or rather, take control of the situation. But, I'm beginning to realize that all of this is happening for a reason. (God, I hope so.) And part of the purpose is the process itself. If there were ever a clearer demonstration that God is in charge, I don't know what it is. He will make the determination as to when Angela will arrive and under what circumstances. He will also give me the strength to deal with it, I hope.*
>
> *I can't. He can. Let Him. I am learning this day by day and trying to live it day by day. I think I have to truly place this in God's hands and try to stop worrying about it. I can keep praying and preparing for it, but this useless worrying is doing no one any good. My mother said something many years ago in a newspaper article about our family. She was asked how she and my father had been able to raise ten daughters and do it so well. She said, "I think God gives you what you can handle." I guess this may apply here as well. He gave me what He thought I could handle. I hope He is right.*

I also spent a great deal of time thinking about heaven. Before Angela, heaven had been a vague concept, a place where everyone is happy and life is perfect. I had been content with that vision, but now I wanted details. I now imagined heaven as a place where you rejoin your family and spend eternity with them.

One day Molly asked me a question about Angela and heaven: "Will Angela still be a baby in heaven or will she be a big girl when I get to heaven?"

Automatically I responded, "Of course she will still be a baby in heaven. She will be just as we remember her."

Satisfied, Molly went back to her crayons and coloring book. Rattled, I did some fast praying. "Please, dear God, let her remain the infant I give back to you." It was the only prayer I could pray. I needed to believe Angela would stay the same. I could not bear the thought of her growing up in heaven without me. I needed to believe she would still be the baby I remembered, as much as I needed to believe that everyone I knew who had died would be just as I remembered when I saw them again. Besides not having aged, all of their problems would have been resolved and they would be perfect again. I knew now that I truly believed in heaven because I had to believe that I would see my Angela again.

While my belief in heaven was secure, my belief in the God who lived in heaven was on shakier ground. I have always believed in God and also believed that He is a good and forgiving God. Now, I could not understand why He was letting all of this happen to me. I felt like I did not deserve it. I did not think I had been a particularly bad person deserving punishment. It just did not seem fair. I had read enough to know that an experience like this can destroy some people's belief in God. I contemplated the idea of turning my back on God, since I felt like He had turned his back on me. I concluded early on, however, that if I turned my back on God, what did I have left? Who could I turn to? Who would be the anchor in my life?

After months of asking God to make my baby healthy, to make the tests turn out well, to perform a miracle in my life, I finally just turned my every fear and concern over to Him. I finally learned how to pray. I learned to stop asking God to bring about some particular outcome and instead to start asking God to help me handle whatever happened.

This shift marked a major turning point in my life. I had always had this vague sense that God did not interfere in the day-to-day actions of our lives, and this sense was heightened as time went on. I believed that God had a general plan but did not really concentrate on any one particular situation at the expense of another. When God "answered" prayers, He was simply bringing about what was already a part of His plan. He was not necessarily giving a specific prayer special attention. I believed in miracles, but I did not believe they happened as often as people wanted them to happen.

By accepting the inevitable and praying that God would help me get through it, I finally realized the true power of prayer. God's help would come not necessarily by changing the situation but by helping me accept it and go through it. Finally, I had found my comfort zone, the safe place where I could stay for the next few months until Angela was born, the place where I could function in my work world and family world and still be in my Angela world.

VII
- LIVING AGAIN -

One day in my seventh month of pregnancy, I was sitting on the couch in our sunroom folding clothes and listening to music. Although I tried to concentrate on the task at hand, my thoughts inevitably turned to Angela. Just then, a song came on the radio that unleashed a flood of memories: Anne Murray's *Could I Have This Dance?* It is one of my all-time favorite songs and had been part of a medley of songs that Bryan and I had chosen for our first dance at our wedding. As I remembered that day, I could not help but think of how happy I had been, happy and in so many ways completely carefree. What could we possibly have had to worry about back then? Our jobs, our new marriage, where we were going to settle down: all those things seem to pale in comparison to what we were facing today. I felt the music invite me to dance, as though it were mocking the fact that I would never get to lead my little Angela in a dance around the room. I would never get to have her put her tiny foot on mine (as Molly had) and gently waltz her around the floor. More painfully, I would never get to watch her dance at her own wedding.

Slowly, without much of an idea of what I was doing, I started to sway back and forth with the music. Soon, I was moving about the room with my arms wrapped around my middle and hugging my daughter as if she were in my arms. The realization that this would be the only way I would ever dance with Angela alive brought tears to my eyes. I did not care about the image I presented or the ungainliness of my gait—I just wanted to dance. As one song faded into another, I became lost in the moment. Time was suspended, and everything else ceased to exist except my beautiful baby, cradled gently in my arms, sharing my love of dancing in the only way I knew how, in the only way our situation would allow. God seemed to wrap his arms around us as if shielding us from any interruptions. I finally collapsed in the chair, tired but exhilarated. I felt like I had triumphed over my despair and uncertainty, if only for a short time. I was going to dance with my daughter Angela and sing to her and just sit and hold her. I was going to take my moments whenever I could. I was going to enjoy my daughter no matter what the circumstances. I was going to live again.

After that first Angela moment, I was determined to create Angela moments whenever I could.

One night I was doing one of my favorite things, reading to Molly. Usually she would sit on my lap, but the size of my stomach prevented her from doing so. Sitting close to me instead, Molly was listening intently as I read another Berenstain Bears adventure. All of a sudden, Molly started laughing and reached over and patted my stomach. Angela moved right then and Molly said, "Mommy, Angela is laughing too!" I gathered Molly closer to me and held on for a minute, afraid to let her see the tears in my eyes. I was so grateful that Molly could incorporate Angela so easily into our routine. At that moment it occurred to me that this was the only way I was going to have both of my girls in my lap at the same time. I hugged Molly so tight she protested. From that day forward, I treasured every opportunity to hold my two girls in my arms.

VIII
- THE BEGINNING OF THE END -

On Monday, November 14, 1994, I went to my office intending to work that day and the next. Angela was going to be induced on Thursday, and I wanted to take Wednesday off to prepare physically for her birth.

After lunch on Monday, I started having regular contractions. I left work at 5:00 and timed the contractions all the way home. They were coming five minutes apart. *Okay, this might be it,* I thought. *It figures, the one thing I thought I had some control over - picking the date - was going to be taken away.* I was not ready. I did not know if I would be ready in two days, but I knew for sure I was not ready now. Once home, Bryan helped me time the contractions. They were very regular, occurring every five minutes and lasting about forty seconds each.

We decided that this might be it, so Bryan started getting our things together. I went upstairs to shower and wash my hair. In the shower, the contractions stopped. Bryan and I spent a rather anxious night, but the contractions did not return with any regularity. When Tuesday dawned I decided to work at home. Once I finished up with my secretary at 5:00, I could finally place the professional part of my life on hold and concentrate entirely on the most important part of my life.

Hoping to distract me for a few hours, my mom and dad called that evening and asked if I wanted to go to dinner with them to celebrate my aunt's birthday. After telling them I was not quite up to it, Mom said that she and Dad would stop by after dinner with a christening gown they had purchased for Angela. I mumbled an okay and hung up the phone as the tears I had held in check all day returned. My sister Kathleen called a little while later and said she would be over some time that evening. Although some people in my situation would have preferred to be left alone, I wanted and needed the company. I had been too alone with my thoughts and fears for almost nine months, and that was long enough. I needed to be with my extended family.

Mom and Dad arrived shortly after 7:00 p.m. As promised, Mom brought a pure white, lacy christening gown, so delicate and soft with a simple white slip and bonnet to match. Mom also brought a little white undershirt and tiny white socks. Aunt Anne sent a crocheted ivory blanket and white satin picture frame. It was so hard, looking at these beautiful things and knowing that Angela would be buried in them. I cried, Mom cried, and Molly told us not to cry. Kathleen arrived and we sat and talked until 9:00.

Everyone left, and I got Molly ready for bed. Bryan then went to his weekly night of basketball. He needed to keep to his routine. This was his way of coping. He needed to do something physical, something to burn away his frustration and fear. Later that night, my sister Celeste called to let me know everyone was thinking about me and praying for Angela.

Wednesday, November 16, began with a doctor's appointment. Bryan decided not to accompany me but instead to leave work early in the afternoon. At the doctor's office they told me to be at the hospital by 9:00 a.m. on Thursday so they could start the Pitocin, a hormone used to initiate labor and to control bleeding after delivery. My doctor estimated that Angela would not be born before 3:00 or 3:30 p.m. He ended the appointment by saying, "Let's get this thing going so we can get all of this behind us." For me, I knew that getting "this thing going" was going to be much faster than the "getting this all behind us."

Bryan came home about an hour after me with a fast-food lunch in hand. As we were finishing up our lunch, my sister Mary Pat arrived. She brought the ingredients for hot spiced cider and set to work preparing it. It was delicious. We sat around and talked all afternoon, mostly about things in general, anything but tomorrow. I remember looking at the clock repeatedly. I would look and think, *It's 2:00 now and I wonder if at 2:00 tomorrow Angela will have been born. Will she still be alive, will she be stillborn, or, will I still be in labor?* I suddenly forgot how delicious the cider was.

Mary Pat left around 8:00 after promising to pick up Molly from school the next day and bring her to the hospital. Bryan helped get Molly ready for bed, and I took a sleeping pill and drifted off to sleep at 9:30. I woke up at 3:00 a.m. and could not get back to sleep. I gave up at 5:00. I sat on the edge of the bed and hugged my baby. I put my arms around my stomach in a gesture that had become so familiar. Angela kept moving so I tried to settle her down by rubbing my stomach. I wanted to talk to her. I hoped that by rubbing my stomach I could get her to settle down so she could listen to me. I realized this would probably be our last time together, just her and me. I tried to tell her how much I loved her. I knew, most likely, that I would never feel her move in my arms outside the womb, so I hugged her as tightly as I could and rocked her back and forth.

With tears running down my cheeks, I told Angela that I was sorry for what was going to happen. For I knew the relief I sought, the relief every expectant mother seeks at the end of her pregnancy, would most likely mean the end of Angela's life. I kept telling her that she would be happy in heaven, that in heaven she would be perfect and not the victim of a mangled body and mind. I said that no matter what she looked like she was perfect in my eyes. I told Angela that God would be waiting for her and would take care of her until I joined her. I knew she did not understand, but I hoped that one day when we met in heaven, she would recognize my voice. I hoped that she would know that I was her mother and how badly I had wanted her to live, and how much I wanted her to be my little girl. I concluded by whispering, "I love you, sweetheart."

IX
- NEVER ENOUGH TIME -

Molly could not have been more excited when Thursday finally arrived. As Bryan helped her get ready for school, she kept saying, "Is this the day that Angela will be born?" I told her it was but tried to gently remind her about Angela's problems and that we probably would not be bringing her home from the hospital. Molly said, "I know Mom, I know. But can't you hardly wait to see her?" For a moment, I could not speak. Despite all the problems, Molly saw Angela as the new baby she could not wait to meet. She voiced what my heart had been telling me all along. Through tears I told her that I too could hardly wait to see Angela.

I could not help but compare this trip to the hospital to the one we took on the morning of August 9, 1989, when Molly came into the world. I was in labor and in a great deal of pain, but I was so happy that I was going to have my baby. We did not know anything about her, except that everything appeared to be fine. I could not wait to be a mother.

On this trip, I assumed my now-familiar position of hugging my stomach, trying to give Angela my warmth and protection. It was my desperate attempt to create memories for the days ahead. I was so afraid she would die during the delivery and I would never get to see her and hold her while she was still living. Now that the end of my journey was near, it was inordinately important to me to see her alive, if only for a short time. I knew she was still alive within me because she moved frequently. I asked her to hold on for a little while longer. I asked the Blessed Mother to intercede on my behalf. Then, because I felt like I did not have anything original to say to God, I just kept praying over and over, "Please help me handle this. Please help me get through this."

Bryan dropped me off at the entrance to the hospital and joined me at Admissions after parking the car. Ms. Reed, the woman handling my admission, barely glanced at me before handing me a bunch of papers to sign. As she went over the papers, she kept repeating they were just routine forms authorizing the delivery of our baby. I asked Ms. Reed if she had on record anything about our baby's condition. This time she actually looked up at me and said, "Condition?" I told her our baby had Trisomy 18 and would probably die during or right after her birth. This time Ms. Reed looked right through me and without a trace of emotion said, "I see."

I felt all the composure I had so carefully maintained for the past few months evaporate in an instant. Instead of crying, I wanted to lash out at her. I stared at her, wanting to confront her. She just handed me more forms to sign. I wanted to tell her that the forms did not matter because Angela was going to die, but I went back to my Angela world and said nothing. Then she asked if we had a pediatrician for our baby. I told her that we had one for our six-year-old daughter, but under the circumstances, I did not think Angela would need one. She still did not seem to get it. The last straw was when she told me that the hospital would not release our baby to us unless we took her home in a car seat. I wanted to shout, *They will be releasing a body not a baby!* but I felt Bryan's hand on my shoulder. He gave it a squeeze as if to say, *Calm down. We'll deal with this later.* I took a deep breath, composed myself, and initialed the form. It was not Ms. Reed's fault — it was not anyone's fault — it just was.

Finally, Ms. Reed put two identification bracelets on me and told me to go to the third-floor labor and delivery area. As we were leaving Admissions, I ran into one of my aunts. When I saw her and knew she had come down to be with us, I started crying. I told her how much I appreciated her coming and that Mom and Dad would be along shortly. Bryan told her that he would escort her upstairs after I was properly checked in.

When we checked in on the third floor, they sent me to a large corner delivery room with a welcoming atmosphere. It was not like the sterile room I had occupied when I was in labor with Molly. This made me feel a little better. As I was getting into my hospital gown, I could hear Bryan asking the nurses if they knew about our special circumstances. Apparently, they did not, and he quickly brought them up to speed. When I came out of the bathroom, I met my labor and delivery nurse. She asked me about the baby and if we had named her. Bryan had to answer her question because suddenly I could not talk. I just started crying. My nurse just hugged me and told me she would do whatever she could to help me through this.

My doctor arrived and started the intravenous drip at 9:45 and the Pitocin at 10:00. My mom and dad and two of my aunts came up shortly thereafter. I told them they could stay as long as they wanted. A few minutes later my sister Kathleen arrived, followed closely by my best friend LeeAnn and my sister Eileen. There was a Mass in the hospital chapel at 11:00, which many of our family members decided to attend.

My doctor checked in periodically to see how I was progressing. He had broken my water shortly after 10:00. I tried to stay upbeat, worrying that if I seemed too depressed my doctor would think I regretted my decision to continue the pregnancy. In later conversations, I was surprised to hear, it turned out we were each trying to keep a brave face for the other.

At 11:00 I was dilated three centimeters. I asked for an epidural, which I received at 11:20. This took a little of the edge off the pain and I relaxed somewhat. At 11:30 everyone returned from Mass and it looked like a regular family gathering. Every time they came and went I thought how normal their lives were in comparison to mine. I went from being scared, to apprehensive, to tired. By this time my sisters Celeste, Susie, and Rosemary had arrived. This may seem like a crowd, and actually it was, but it was my family. As the second oldest of ten children I was accustomed to a crowd and quite comfortable with it. Just that day the hospital had opened a grieving room where families could have some privacy in difficult circumstances. My family traveled back and forth from there. Bryan's family kept in touch with us by phone. We thought Angela's birth might be too hard on Jessica, so she stayed with her mother and kept Angela in her prayers.

A few minutes past noon my discomfort increased and a nurse sent for the anesthesiologist. He arrived at 12:30 and gave me another dose of medicine. This was nothing like Molly's delivery. Besides the obvious difference in the outcome of the deliveries, this labor was physically more uncomfortable. I had heard that induced deliveries are more painful than natural ones, but I had not really focused on that. It would have been just one more thing to worry about.

By 1:30 I had a really full house. My pain was increasing, and I could feel the contractions getting harder. Molly had not arrived yet, and I was concerned that she might not get to the hospital in time.

At 1:45 I told my nurse that I wanted to push. She checked me and announced that I was ten centimeters and the baby was coming. She called for another nurse and told her to get Dr. Wallace immediately. I grabbed the rails on the side of the bed and told Bryan that it really hurt and I had to push. He told me to hold on until my doctor arrived. I felt like I was in too much pain for everything to be all right. I worried that something else was happening to the baby. It was 1:50.

Suddenly everyone was moving. My doctor arrived, and my nurse cleared my family from the room. The bed was torn apart, a big light came from the ceiling, and the doctors and nurses suited up. My doctor told me to grab my legs and start pushing with the next contraction. I did as he asked, but I felt exhausted. I had no energy. The pain was intense, and I felt like pushing was not relieving it. I pushed as hard as I could and then told Bryan I could not do it. They told me I was doing fine and to keep on pushing. I pushed again, and after some intense pain and burning I felt some relief as Angela appeared. My doctor asked me if I wanted her on my stomach, and I said yes. I was crying from relief and I was scared to ask if she was alive. I kept saying, "Is she breathing?" And Bryan made my heart fill up when he said, "She's breathing! She's alive!" The next few minutes were the most wonderful and heartbreaking minutes of my life. I kept looking at her and touching her and thanking God for her birth. I was so grateful she was alive and so happy to finally see my precious little angel.

My nurse took Angela from me, put a cap on her head, cleaned off her face, and wrapped her in a blanket. Then, she handed Angela back to me. I said, "Hello, sweetheart. I'm so glad to see you. You are so beautiful." I kissed her cheek and hugged her close. Bryan held her too. We kept hugging her. Bryan started crying with me and told Angela over and over how beautiful she was. We took lots of pictures, as if taking them would somehow help preserve her life.

A nun from the hospital, Sister Andrea, came in and asked if we wanted Angela baptized. We said yes. She said she could do it for us, or we could ask the hospital chaplain to do it. Since my doctor was still stitching me, and I knew time was precious, I asked Sister Andrea to perform the baptism. She asked the nurse for some water, but I told her that I had some water from Lourdes. She said, "Wonderful." Sister Andrea proceeded with the baptism, saying, "Angela, I baptize you in the name of the Father, and of the Son, and of the Holy Spirit." We blessed ourselves and blessed our beautiful little daughter. Then Bryan and I hugged her together, just the three of us, our little family, our little baby. I was afraid to hug her too tight or to hold her too close or to kiss her lips. I was so afraid I would steal what little breath she had in her. We kept telling her how much we loved her and how happy we were to see her.

A few minutes later I agreed to give Angela to my nurse so she could weigh and measure her. Bryan went with the nurse, a few feet away, and then promptly came back. "She's gone. She's passed away." Somehow, while we were holding her, she died. I just looked at him, and the floodgates opened. *It's not fair. It wasn't long enough.* I knew she was going to die but I needed a little more time. There was so much I had to tell her, so much I wanted her to know. But she was gone and we were still here and so alone. We just held each other and cried. My heart was breaking.

The neonatologist who was attending the birth came over and said, "Your daughter was not in any pain, and she did not struggle." She continued saying that Angela had all the conditions associated with Trisomy 18, so that we could be assured that the early diagnosis was consistent with her findings. She told me she was very sorry. Then she handed Angela back to me.

I hugged her as tightly as I could as if willing my life into hers. I told her, "I love you, my little baby doll." I rubbed my cheek against hers, and for the first time I kissed her on her soft little lips. I knew I could not hurt her breathing, for she would not be taking any more breaths. I touched her hands and felt the softness of her newborn skin. I kept thinking how beautiful she was. She had dark hair and a cute little nose. I never saw her eyes. Later, Bryan told me that she had opened her eyes once and they were gray, and then she had closed them forever.

X
- My "Save" Baby -

I knew my family was waiting patiently to meet Angela. I took a deep breath and told Bryan to ask them to come in. By this time my youngest sisters, Cecilia and Liz, had arrived, in addition to everyone else. They all came in and took turns holding our beautiful baby daughter. All I could say was, "Can you believe how beautiful she is?" My mother's first words were, "Ah, Sweetheart, isn't she a doll!" Tears, hugs, and kisses filled the room. Cameras clicked and flashes went off as everyone tried to preserve the moment.

Before long, Molly arrived. She practically skipped into the room holding a balloon and wearing a big smile. She stopped short, and her smile turned to a serious expression as she took in the trappings of the room. I am not sure what she was thinking, but clearly she was not prepared for me to be in a hospital bed with an intravenous needle in my arm and a doctor and nurse standing nearby.

When I tried to coax Molly over to my bed to meet her little sister, she just hung back and wanted Bryan to pick her up. I said, "Come on over, honey. It's okay." But Molly needed a few minutes to get her bearings. Finally, after what seemed like an eternity, she approached my bed and took a look at her little sister. "Is she dead?" she asked. I nodded my head, too afraid to speak lest my tears start again and scare Molly. "She's so little," Molly said softly. I asked her if she wanted to hold Angela, but she refused. I asked her if she wanted to climb up in bed with me and give me a hug and kiss. She hesitated, and I told her how much I needed a hug. Molly did not know how desperately I needed my living daughter to hug me the way my new little daughter never would. Molly finally complied, and I thanked God for her.

A few minutes later, our parish priest, Father Lee Fangmeyer, entered the room. He was so calm and reassuring as he talked to Bryan and me, to my mother and father, and to the rest of the family. Two of my brothers-in-law walked in next, ballooning the number of family present to fifteen. Other than the fact that Angela was not alive, the scene resembled many of the gatherings we had to welcome a new grandchild. Despite the tragic circumstances, my family came to do whatever it could to help Bryan,

Molly, and me celebrate Angela's all-too-brief life. I was never prouder of my family.

I watched Molly as she worked her way around the room, getting closer to whomever was holding Angela, not quite ready to do so herself. Then she went over to my mother and whispered something in her ear. My mother nodded and asked my sister Eileen to let Molly hold Angela. Molly put her arms out and then stared down quietly at Angela. "Can I take her over to my mom?" Molly asked.

As if on cue, the hum of quiet conversations stopped. Everyone watched as Molly gathered Angela close in her arms, safe and secure. Tears slid down my mother's cheeks as she watched her two grandchildren start across the room.

Molly walked carefully over to my bed. She asked me if Angela had arms and legs. Angela was wrapped tightly in a blanket, and all Molly or anyone could see was her delicate face and little head and neck. I took Angela from Molly, and together we opened the blanket. Apart from Angela's little elevated chest from the diaphragmatic hernia, her twisted right foot, and her two clenched fists, there were no visible signs of Trisomy 18.

"Mom, look!" Molly was so excited she could hardly get the words out. "Angela has a birthmark, just like me!" I could not believe it. High up on the right side of her chest, Angela had a strawberry birthmark, in the exact same spot as Molly's.

I hugged both of them and said, "You're right, Molly. She's your sister. She looks just like you, right down to the birthmark." Inwardly, I thanked God for this little miracle. Although I had examined Angela right after they handed her to me, I had not noticed the birthmark. I was so happy that Molly had been the one to discover it.

At about that time my sister Maureen, who lived in San Francisco—the only one of the ten of us who lived outside the immediate area—called to share the moment. She kept telling me how proud she was of me. I told her what I kept telling everyone with me in the room. Seeing Angela alive, holding her, telling her I loved her, had made everything worthwhile, all the grief, uncertainty, and confusion. The decision to proceed with the pregnancy had been the correct one. I now had the face of my infant daughter forever etched in my memory. After four miscarriages, which left me with nothing but empty dreams and faceless memories, I finally had a new daughter to hold, if only for a little while.

Father Fangmeyer gathered everyone together for a blessing. We all prayed for strength in the coming days. The only way I was able to get through that day was to concentrate on the moment. I could not begin to think about the next day or even that night; I just immersed myself in the present. I knew that every passing minute was taking me further away from the minutes just after Angela's birth. I did not want to think about how brief my time with her would be. I just wanted to exist. I knew Angela was in heaven now, looking down on us and praying for us. I would need every one of those prayers in the days ahead.

Shortly after Angela was born, it occurred to me that I had passed her from my hands to God's hands. If I did not keep thinking about her that way, I would not have been able to leave the hospital. I kept looking at my little girl and thinking how peaceful and calm she looked. Her face bore no signs of struggle or pain. This was my focus, not that she was dead or that I would soon have to go home without her.

My gaze departed from Angela when some of my sisters, however reluctantly, started gathering up their things, preparing to leave. Celeste thought that Molly might want to go home with her so she could spend the night with her cousins. That was my original plan, but I was not quite ready to let Molly go. She, however, was ready, and I let her kiss Angela for the last time. At the door to my hospital room she waved good-bye and blew me a kiss. Then she was gone. I felt like someone pulled a plug and let all the air out of me. I was sorry to see Molly go but relieved that I did not have to pretend anymore.

Not long after Molly left with Celeste, my sister Susie asked if I wanted to put Angela in her christening gown so we could take a picture of her. My hands were shaking from the epidural so I did not think I could do it, but, thankfully, my nurse said she would love to help. Susie took Angela over to a side table and, with my mother's and my nurse's help, dressed her in the delicate christening gown. They brought her back to me and laid her on my bed with her ivory blanket underneath her. Because she was only four pounds, eleven ounces, the christening gown, as pure as her soul, seemed to swirl around her like a cloud. She looked like an angel. One picture shows my hand near Angela's two clinched fists and my mother's hand putting a Miraculous Medal on Angela's gown. I see my mother's hand weathered with age, my hand gently caressing Angela's arm, and Angela's hands clenched tightly, unable to open up and hold either of our hands. It is my only picture of the three of us.

The more I looked at Angela, the more she reminded me of a doll my sister Mary Pat had received for Christmas when she was a child. Back then, my mother would encourage us to ask for a "save doll." The idea was not to play with it but to put it away and save it as a keepsake doll, maybe to give to our own daughter one day. Mary Pat's save doll had a white lace bonnet and white lace gown and came wrapped in an embroidered white blanket. Angela looked like Mary Pat's save doll; for me, she was my "save baby." She was the one to preserve forever in the condition in which she was received, the one not to be enjoyed because she has a different destiny. My save baby.

XI
- EMPTY ARMS -

After a few more pictures, my parents decided to go home. My sister Liz, ever vigilant of Mom and Dad, answered my unspoken question, saying, "I'll take care of Mom and Dad. God bless you, Nancy." This left my sisters Mary Pat and Eileen with Bryan, Angela, and me. It was 6:00 and growing dark outside, and Bryan wanted us to get ready to go to the room in which I would be spending the night. I later learned from Bryan that he was afraid that Angela's body would start to stiffen, a memory he (and I) did not want.

My nurse told me that after I had settled in my room, the floor nurse would bring Angela back to me for as long as I wanted. I looked down at my infant daughter and said good-bye. I hugged her as tightly as I could, and, after giving her a kiss, I handed her to the nurse. Very gently, she placed Angela's body on a table and called to another nurse to help her. She kindly asked the nurse to stay with Angela while she accompanied me to my overnight room. As I was wheeled out of the room, I looked back one last time to see my daughter's body resting on the table. I wanted to scream, jump out of the wheel chair, and take her with me. I wanted to tell them not to leave her by herself, that she would be afraid without me. *She is not used to being alone. I've always been with her. I don't want her to be afraid.*

Rather than say anything, however, I just put my head down and hugged my hands to my heart. I thought, *Angela's here with me now, in my heart. She's not on that table. She's with God in heaven.* Despite these thoughts, the tears just flowed down my cheeks. The raw pain of leaving her was more than I could bear. She truly was gone.

Even with all I had done to concentrate on the fact that Angela's soul had left her body and was now in heaven, it was incredibly difficult to leave her behind. I appreciated how my nurse asked another nurse to keep watch over Angela's body when we had to leave. It was wonderful how she treated my daughter's still, lifeless, tiny body with dignity and love. I still have the image burned in my mind of Angela's body, clad in her white christening gown, lying all alone on a cold metal table. I do believe that God kept me from being hysterical, or maybe it was Angela herself, who had already taken up permanent residence in my memory, in my heart, and in my soul.

The wheelchair ride to my overnight room took forever. All I could hear was the sound of babies crying and making noise. I passed happy relatives with flowers and balloons in their hands and thought, *This isn't fair. It just isn't fair.*

When I reached my hospital room, I was exhausted. I wished I had prevailed upon my doctor to let me go home. I had decided not to have Angela's body brought back to me. I knew I was not going to say a goodbye a second time. I knew that if I asked to see her again, I would lose control. The thought of losing control of my emotions terrified me, which is why my sudden and frequent tears throughout my pregnancy troubled me so much. But part of my whole experience with Angela involved learning how to relinquish control. This was a tough lesson for someone who had lived for years under the illusion of complete control.

I had spent five or six hours after Angela's death reminding myself that I was only holding a body; that her soul, her essence, her spirit, had traveled to heaven. I also reminded myself that part of Angela's soul had taken up permanent residence in my heart and in the hearts of all the people who were able to see and love her. I was so happy to have had this time with her, even if she were not alive. I was able to look at her, hug her close, and examine her to see whom she resembled. I was able to let my family hold her and know that she was a real person, a real baby before she became our little angel.

Soon it was 10:00, and Mary Pat and Eileen prepared to leave. At this time one of my brothers-in-law, a doctor, stopped by after his hospital shift. With his kindness and empathy, Tony, my sister Cecilia's husband, fills up a room and comforts everyone. He told us how sorry he was about Angela. He said how difficult it is to be a member of a profession that experiences significant medical advances every day and yet cannot save all the babies. Unbeknownst to me, he had been in contact throughout the day with my doctors and the staff, keeping tabs on my progress even though he could not be there. What a wonderful family Angela was missing.

Later, when Bryan and I were alone at last, Bryan tried, unsuccessfully, to get comfortable in the room's only chair. Finally, I told him to go home and get some sleep. He refused at first, until I told him that my doctor had left instructions that I could take a sleeping pill.

Bryan departed for home, and I began to get ready for bed. I was bleeding heavily and experiencing uncomfortable post-labor cramping. I had not remembered all this pain or bleeding after Molly's birth. I only remembered the love, satisfaction, and pride that enveloped me like a warm blanket. I did not want to go to sleep after Molly was born because I did not want to miss a single minute of her development. Now, all I had was physical discomfort and an intense desire to hold my baby in my arms. There was no baby, no hugs, no midnight feedings — nothing to show for all we had gone through.

At this point I almost reconsidered my earlier decision not to see Angela again. I could not bear to think of her in some cold basement, by herself, wondering why I was not coming to get her, why I had left her all alone. But I knew that when I said goodbye to her, I had to start thinking of her in heaven, not still a part of the little body that had failed to keep her alive. Hence my decision not to ask them to bring her back to me. If I had done so, I might never have been able to give her back. I would have held her forever. She had only been alive for ten minutes, and I had only held her for the next few hours. What parent could possibly crowd a life-time with a child into a few short hours? There just was not enough time.

Some parents in my situation would have had their child brought back to them or visited him or her at the funeral home, but I knew I had only so much reserve strength. I had to make some decisions in advance and stick to them. This was all a manifestation of my desire to be in control of each aspect of my life.

The night seemed endless. The hospital staff insisted on coming in to take my blood pressure and temperature every four hours. It was not conducive to sleeping, even with a sleeping pill.

The next morning I woke up early and prepared to go home. The kind morning nurse said that she had lost a baby late in her second trimester. She told me how sorry she was and encouraged me to take my time getting through the months ahead. Bryan arrived shortly thereafter and brought some of my favorite hot tea. Then my doctor stopped by to sign my release. He brought his partner with him. I realized that it was extremely rare for both of them to make rounds together and appreciated their vist. They told me how well I had handled everything and that, physically, I should recover without too much trouble. They asked if I needed anything, and I wanted to say I needed my baby, something I knew they would understand. Instead, I told them again, as I had told my doctor yesterday, that seeing Angela alive and holding her for those few minutes had made everything worthwhile. I reaffirmed how glad I was to have gone forward with the pregnancy.

I left the hospital by wheelchair, and I could not help but think of the contrast with my last time leaving this hospital after giving birth to Molly. I was proud, excited, and incredibly happy. This time I just kept my head down and tried not to make eye contact with anyone. I kept my hands in my lap, so poignantly aware of my empty arms.

While I waited near the hospital entrance, Bryan went to get the car. Beside me a woman wait in a wheelchair, holding her newborn bundled in pink. Pink balloons also surrounded her, so I figured she had a little girl. I willed myself to look away and kept thinking, *Just get me home. Just get me out of here.* There were so many times I could feel my grip on my control slipping away. I feared falling into an abyss, an abyss from which I might never emerge. I could not deal with that, so I concentrated on everything but what was happening to me.

It was a rainy day, and I watched the windshield wipers go back and forth on the taxicab parked at the entrance to the hospital. One wiper had a piece of paper stuck to it. I counted how many times the wipers went back and forth before the paper worked itself free and slid off the windshield. I did not allow myself to think of Angela's body in the morgue, her lifeless body growing ever more cold and stiff. Instead, I put my hands over my heart as if keeping her there, as if by doing something physical, something visible, I could show the world where my daughter really was.

When we left the hospital, the rain grew more intense, making it a dark, gloomy day. We rode home in silence. I clutched my stomach, which just one day before had held my little daughter, and the tears started anew. I felt so alone, so empty, so depressed. In my mind, I went over and over those brief ten minutes of my baby's life. I tried to will myself to think of anything positive to console myself, but I could not come up with a single thing. *It was just so unfair, so unjust.* I just sat there in the car staring out the window, wrapped completely in my misery.

Once home I went straight to bed. There was something reassuring about being back at home, in my bed, where everything was familiar. My sister Mary Pat came over to stay with me while Bryan went to the funeral home to make final arrangements. Relieved that he was tending to such things, I fell asleep thinking of empty arms and broken hearts.

When I awoke two hours later, Mary Pat offered to make some soup for me. I was not really hungry, but I accepted the offer anyway. After Mary Pat left my room, reality set in once again. Here I was, alone in my bedroom, with all the appearances of just having had a baby, and yet, no baby. There was no baby in my stomach, no baby in my arms, no baby sleeping in the bassinet. I started crying inconsolably. I was desperate. At that moment I realized I had prepared myself so well for Angela's birth and death that I had neglected to think of the day after. That had seemed so overwhelming. I had planned out the day of Angela's birth, thereby keeping myself under control. I had things to do to occupy my time and attention. And now, the day after was here. The next few days, the next few months, stretched out endlessly before me. I did not have a clue what to do, how to act, how to get myself out of bed in the morning. I did not know how I would be able to go on.

XII
- She Was Real -

I woke up early on Monday, November 21, the day of Angela's funeral. At first, I was a little disoriented. I could not remember how many days it had been since Angela's death. As usual, I had not slept well. The clock read 6:15. I laid back down in bed and mentally reviewed what would occur. Father Fangmeyer was going to do a graveside service beginning at 11:00. I expected no more than thirty people to attend, mostly family. I had wanted a full Mass of Christian Burial, but our pastor had advised against it. He said that such a Mass is for someone who has lived a long life and needs the prayers of the living to get to heaven. Angela had been baptized and had no ability to commit sin, so she was already in heaven and not really in need of further prayer. I wish I had persisted and said that I needed the Mass, with its prayers, rituals, familiarity, and time to grieve. Angela may not have needed it, but I sure did. Thankfully, I later discovered a memorial Mass for our special circumstances called the Mass of Angels.

I listened carefully and heard rain falling. *Perfect,* I thought. *Just perfect.* I looked over at Bryan, who was still sleeping. I listened to his rhythmic breathing and thought, *I'm glad he is still asleep. This has been hard on him, harder, I think, than he expected. I know it was much harder than I expected.* I had hoped that since we were so well prepared for what was to happen that somehow it would be easier for us. We had good pictures, and good memories of the day Angela was born and died, but that did not make it any easier. She still died. All I had were pictures and memories.

I was still bleeding and bloated from Angela's birth. My breast milk had come in the day before, and it just added to the pain of losing my daughter. With Molly my milk had come in late, and so I had to start her on formula. This time, even without the stimulation of breast feeding, my milk had come in, another cruel reminder of my loss.

I got out of bed, made a cup of tea, and took a shower. I took my time getting Molly ready, combing her hair into pigtails, and helping her with her red plaid skirt and turtleneck. She had never been to a funeral and, as usual, was full of questions. She wanted to know if she would be able to see Angela again and hold her. Shaking my head, I forced myself to think of Angela in heaven and not in the awful box soon to be lowered into the ground.

Bryan's parents arrived at 9:00 for the service, which had been moved indoors due to the weather. I had no energy to entertain them, so I stayed in my room. I wore a brown turtleneck sweater and my favorite tweed jacket. Looking in the mirror, I marveled that I had gone through the birth and death of my daughter but did not look any different. Outwardly, I was the same person I had been before my pregnancy. But inside, I was forever changed. Any innocence I had carried into my forties was gone for good. *Bad things happen to good people; babies sometimes die. I* kept telling myself it would be over soon.

Although I had tried to prepare myself, the sight of her little coffin was heartbreaking. It looked so small and lonely. It was covered with tiny pink and white carnations. We placed an eight inch by ten inch framed picture of Angela in her christening gown next to the coffin. It was there to validate her birth to all those attending the service, especially those who had not seen her at the hospital. I wanted to scream out, *See, I told you she was real! I told you I had a baby! I really did have a baby, and she did exist! Angela did exist!*

The memorial chapel was much more crowded than I had anticipated. It was filled to overflowing with sixty or seventy people. I was both surprised and grateful. The presence of so many relatives and friends helped to validate Angela's short life.

Our parish priest spoke about the sanctity of life and lifted up Bryan and me as good parents for giving Angela her only chance at life. I did not feel like a good parent right then. I felt like the parent of a dead child. At the end of the service, my sister Rosemary read a poem written by a family friend whose niece had been stillborn. The poem was beautiful and heartrending, yet so appropriate. Despite the tears it generated, it made me feel good, or at least feel better. It put into words so much of what I was thinking, so much of what I was going through. The poem was written for the parents of a dead child and concluded with "I will be waiting for you in heaven." *I hope so,* I thought, because I could not wait to see Angela again.

After the service, everyone stopped to speak with Bryan and me. We hugged and cried and thanked everyone for coming. I kept pointing to Angela's picture and telling everyone how beautiful she was.

My sister Kathleen and her husband, John, had everyone over to their house after the service. I sat in the living room with my book of pictures showing my little daughter's life to everyone who was interested. Celeste and Cecilia sat with me to keep me company. It seemed that many people, however, stayed away from me. They did not know what to say, so they avoided the situation and avoided me at the same time. When it was time to go, I thanked my sister and her husband and clutched my photo album to my heart. I looked around the room and gathered up the two eight by ten framed pictures.

"This is all I have," I said to my sister. "This is all that is left of my baby."

XIII
- No Thanks -

I took two months off for maternity leave. Some people urged me to take the minimum leave of six weeks, thinking it best to get back to work and to life as soon as possible. I had read enough to know that I wanted to take my time to grieve. I was not sure exactly what that meant, but the books said to grieve early or the grief would come back later and be far more powerful. I did not think anything could be more powerful or traumatic than what I was experiencing, but I decided I wanted to go through it now rather than later.

Thanksgiving came one week to the day after Angela's death. The joy of that day was not sufficient to overcome my grief. Our family tradition is for all of us to gather around noon at my sister Kathleen's house. Before I was married, I would spend the night before Thanksgiving at their house and rise early for breakfast and the annual parades on television. After we married, Bryan and I would go over early in the morning and continue the tradition. Bryan would play touch football with my brothers-in-law and some of my cousins. This Thanksgiving, however, I could not bring myself to get out of bed. Bryan took Molly over for the parades and then went to play football. I just stayed in bed and cried.

When Bryan returned, I told him I could not go over for dinner. I had no energy, and I was not thankful for anything. He told me that I needed to go, that my parents needed to have me there, and that everyone else was expecting me to be there. I told him that everyone was expecting me to get better, but I was not. It was going to take a long time. But Bryan insisted that I go. I think my reactions were beginning to scare him. He said Molly would be expecting us and would be upset if we did not come.

Reluctantly, I agreed to go, but not until 3:00, three hours after everyone would have assembled. I wanted to be home when the clock said 2:01, the time of Angela's birth. I needed to relive the moments that were so fresh in my mind. At the appointed time, Bryan and I sat together on our bed and went through the album of pictures. I was heartbroken all over again, but it was worth it. I felt like I had my special time with Angela, our special time together, our Thanksgiving. Bryan sat quietly with me.

I felt God's presence near me. I looked up at a plaque on our wall displaying the poem "The Footprints of God." My eyes arrived at the part that read, "'My precious child,' God answered, 'When your life had pain, I knew;

The single set of footprints were the times I carried you.'" I turned to God and begged Him to carry me. I felt like He was crying with me. A sense of peace came over me and I told Bryan I was ready to go to Thanksgiving dinner.

My family was there waiting for us. Everything was the same as past years, but this time it all seemed to go in slow motion. I made my way to the couch in the family room and sat down beside my Uncle Tommy, who asked me how I was doing. Before I could reply, the tears slipped out. He awkwardly patted my shoulder and went back to watching the football game. My family came in and out of the room, but no one spoke to me. I did not want to make people uncomfortable, but it took all my will power not to cry. I did not have any energy left for conversation.

Thankfully, dinner was ready and we sat down to eat. My dad always leads the prayers. Before we say Grace together, he thanks God for all the blessings our family has enjoyed over the years and, in particular, over the past year. He always concludes this part by welcoming the newest grandchild or son-in-law. That year he began, "God bless Sean" (my sister Susie's son who had arrived in June). Then after a short pause he said, "and Angela."

My heart leapt at the sound of Angela's name. It was so good to hear someone say her name out loud. I was not sure how my dad was going to handle her death, but it was just right. I hugged my hands to my heart and joined in the blessing. Traditionally, my dad follows this prayer by saying, "And now let's say three Hail Marys for the deceased members of the families represented here today." Prior to our marriages, Dad would confine the prayer to the deceased members of our immediate family. Once husbands started showing up, Dad expanded the circle to include them. But that Thanksgiving, when he said, "the deceased members of the families represented here today," I realized that the circle included Angela. My euphoria at hearing her name dissolved at the word "deceased." I struggled through the Hail Marys. I should have been bursting with thankfulness. I should have had a one-week-old baby sleeping in my arms. My head ached from holding back the tears. *I need to be carried, God. I need a little help here.* The earlier peace I had felt at home was nowhere to be found. I guessed that God must be really busy on Thanksgiving.

I tried to eat, and did take some comfort in the food, but I felt so alone. I was surrounded by family who were talking, laughing, and enjoying Thanksgiving dinner. I just wanted to go home and go to bed. When it was over, I went home and mentally marked off my first Thanksgiving without Angela. It was awful, but at least it was over.

XIV
- A LIFELINE -

As the days went by, the burden of Angela's death grew heavier. I had spent the time before her birth and death planning and preparing. Suddenly, I had nothing left to prepare for. That part of my life was over, and I had to go on. Alone.

Though God was with me, I sensed He was going to "let" me move forward, not "lead" me forward. For months, He had taken my hand, put His arm around my shoulder, and led me through each day. Now I felt He was coaxing me to move more on my own again. He would always be there for me, but now I needed to take off the training wheels and ride on my own.

Molly was my reason to get up each day. She still had to go to school; she still had to live her life. If it had not been for her, I would have stayed in bed. I wanted to sleep away my grief. I wanted it to be one year or ten years from the present. I wanted it to be after whatever time it took to get over this incredible grief, sadness, pain, and despair. I wanted my baby back, and if that was not possible, I wanted time to move on and to move away from the present.

During the first two weeks after Angela's death, the arrival of the mail brought a welcome relief. With each delivery, I would receive several sympathy cards and notes. It was one way to keep Angela alive. I would read and cry and remember. But like everything else associated with Angela, the mail stopped coming. I soon grew to hate the mail carrier. I hated that he would only bring me bills and advertisements. It was as if even he was telling me it was time to move on, time to get over Angela and get on with my life. I was not even close to being ready.

Several weeks after Angela's death, I received a letter from Kathleen, the sister of one of my sister's friends, in which she recounted the stillbirth of her daughter, Sophia. The letter was heartbreaking, touching, and *welcome*. Finally, I had encountered someone who knew what I was going through, someone who had walked in my shoes, someone who understood.

In addition to offering her condolences and sharing her feelings with me, Kathleen offered some practical advice:

Put together an album with all the congratulatory cards, ultrasound pictures, your pictures of Angela, the sympathy cards, and mementos from the hospi-

tal. Hopefully, you got a locket of Angela's hair and footprints and hand prints. Find a beautifully decorated box to store all the artifacts associated with Angela's life.

Kathleen also mentioned that she had attended several meetings of a support group called MIS, or Miscarriage, Infant death, and Stillbirth. It was a group that was organized and facilitated by women who had endured these tragedies. The group met once a month at a local hospital, and Kathleen found it to be a safe place to talk about her loss, to heal, and to learn from others. At long last, I had a little hope and some specific things to do.

I also found some hope in a growing collection of visible signs of Angela's life. A friend gave me a guardian angel pin, which I wore every day for months. Even my mother and aunts and some of my sisters wore guardian angel pins in remembrance of Angela. This comforted me greatly.

Bryan gave me a locket engraved with Angela's name and "November 17, 1994." Inside he had placed two tiny pictures of Angela. I hung on to that necklace for dear life. It was a wonderful way to share Angela with everyone. Whenever someone commented on the locket it gave me an opportunity to talk about Angela. Over time, my younger nieces and nephews would ask to see Angela's picture and give her a kiss. Wearing the locket around my neck keeps Angela close to my heart.

On a much larger scale, my office staff decided to send me a pink dogwood tree, which we planted the spring after Angela died. I had read that planting flowers, a bush, or a tree was a good way of creating a lasting memory. The thought of planting something that would outlast our time on earth comforted me greatly. The first year it bloomed was a joyful, therapeutic experience. When we moved from our home five years later, we took the tree with us. I was a little concerned about what I would do if the tree died, but it still blooms every year and everyone knows it is our Angela tree.

The guardian angel pin, the locket, and the dogwood tree helped, but they did not heal me. With each passing day, I missed Angela more, not less. I began to wonder if I would ever find peace.

XV
- RE-ENTRY -

Going back to work was both reassuring and draining. I had not seen most of my staff since Angela's graveside service, though I had received many cards, letters, notes, and phone calls from them immediately following Angela's death. I went back for half days the first week and full days the following week. I decided to leave early on Mondays for the remainder of the school year in order to meet Molly after school. Molly and I had enjoyed our time together for the two months following Angela's birth and I wanted to hold on to that mother-daughter time for a little while longer.

My first day back was heartwarming, exhausting, and ultimately disappointing. I was welcomed back with hugs and pats on the back, but no one really wanted to talk with me. I would walk down a hallway and see a co-worker coming my way. He or she would acknowledge me or wave to me and then quickly duck through a doorway and disappear. When I approached a group of people talking they would make excuses about getting back to work and scatter in every direction. On the few occasions when I mentioned Angela, people would look away and silently wait for someone to change the subject.

Over time, two or three people with whom I was close allowed me to open up and discuss how I was feeling. But this was the rare exception. When I was able to talk to people about why they never brought up Angela, they would say, almost universally, "I didn't want to remind you; I didn't want to make you think about it." My reaction was always the same: "I think about Angela all the time. Don't worry; you won't make me feel worse. It is hard for me these days but it is even harder when you act like Angela never happened, when you act like she didn't exist." I had this huge need to talk about Angela, an incredible desire to validate her existence to everyone.

My office had seen me pregnant several months ago, and though I was back and looking very much as I had before my pregnancy, I was not the same person who had left the office three months earlier. My whole world had changed, and no one understood why I should be any different. And, worse still, everyone wanted to discuss all the problems and concerns of the workplace. These concerns would have been enormously important to me months ago, but now they seemed trivial compared to the trauma I had just endured.

To cope, I practiced something I had read in a book dealing with grief. The author suggested that the one stricken with grief spend a few minutes each day totally focused on her grief. Whether these few minutes fell at the beginning, middle, or end of the day, the critical step was taking time to embrace the grief, and more often, to *wallow* in it. The author believed that these moments of grief would make it possible to function effectively in the real world. At first this technique seemed ridiculous and even impossible. How could I limit my grief? But over time, the process actually began to work. In the beginning, I felt like I was doing the reverse. I would spend most of my time thinking about Angela, sorting through all my feelings, and only marginally participating in the real world. The only way I knew how to hold on to Angela was to think about her.

I would so often retreat from the real world into my Angela world, which consisted primarily of three principal daydreams. In the first one, I would relive the minutes from her birth to her death. I would picture myself in the hospital, my doctor placing Angela on my stomach and her warmth spreading over me like a shield. Then I would pick her up and see her face for the first time. What bliss! Her tiny pug nose so much like Molly's nose, her heart-shaped lips reminiscent of her stepsister Jessica's lips, and just a hint of a curl in her hair so unlike my often unruly mane. Her eyelids closed peacefully, guarding their secret gems, and her cheeks high and full like her father's. Then I would rub my cheek on her cheek and know that only God could create such perfection. I would kiss her and hug her and promise to love her forever. Time was suspended as I slowly went over each detail, one memory at a time.

In the second daydream, I imagined how life might have looked with Angela. This daydream became important to me as Angela's birth and death drifted further into the past. I would recall what I had done with Molly in her first year of life and imagine that I had done those things with Angela. We would go to the park and I would push her contentedly in the baby swing, or we would take a stroller ride through the neighborhood introducing ourselves to all the birds and squirrels we met along the way. Then we would snuggle in the rocking chair silently and peacefully.

In my last daydream I envisioned Angela in heaven. I would picture my grandparents comforting her and rocking her to sleep. Sometimes, I would picture her with the other babies I had lost to miscarriages. These dreams, however, were frustrating as I did not know the gender of these babies and so could barely picture them.

At home on maternity leave, I could indulge in these daydreams. I had large blocks of time which were occupied mostly by grief, and these precious reveries helped ease my pain. I could go freely from my Angela world to the real world as I had done throughout my pregnancy.

Returning to work forced me to shift my focus. My professional responsibilities demanded that I pay attention to the priorities of budget, technology, and workforce issues. I could no longer indulge my desire to live in my Angela world. My only recourse was to exchange my Angela world for what I called my Angela moments. For example, I dedicated the hour commute to and from work to Angela. During most commutes I would talk to her, telling her all my hopes and dreams, and confiding my fears and disappointments. This helped me feel close to her as time marched on.

My return to work served to signal to Bryan and to the rest of the world that I was moving on. For them moving on meant grocery shopping, paying bills, doing housework—everything a full-time wife and working mother was expected to do. But I was not ready to move on; I was still grieving. Everyone thought I was recovering because they wanted and needed me to get better, but I needed more time. I also needed a place to grieve and, just as important, people to grieve with me. My thoughts turned to Kathleen's letter.

XVI
- LIFE SUPPORT -

In late January I attended my first MIS (Miscarriage, Infant death, and Stillbirth) support group. Despite my fragile emotional state, I wanted to see if the group could help me.

Bryan was hardly enthusiastic about going to the meeting. On the ride over he announced that he did not want to talk about Angela. He was going to the meeting to support me, and he expected me to do all the talking. That was fine with me. The meeting was being held in the hospital where Angela had been born. It was my first trip back to the hospital since that day. I clutched my locket to my heart as I walked into the building, knowing that Angela had been with me the last time I took these steps. I almost heard her say, *I'm still here, Mom.*

We arrived at the meeting just before it began. There must have been twenty-five or thirty people in the room. It was a much bigger group than I had expected and my newfound courage faltered. A woman greeted us and seated Bryan and me together. The chairs were arranged in a horse-shoe shape. One of the group leaders asked everyone to take their seats and I remember her saying, "We're sorry you are here tonight. We know you would rather be home with your babies, but we hope we can help you, and that is why we are here." She went on to explain that everyone would get a chance to tell their story. After the three group leaders had given their backgrounds, the group leader who had begun the session said, "Sharing your stories helps form a bond with others who are also in a lot of pain. Sharing can help start the healing process."

I looked at the group leaders and thought, *Okay, they look normal. They got dressed and got here. Maybe they can lead this group. Maybe someday I will be normal again. Maybe someday I will be like them too.* The group leaders shared stories of losses they had suffered several years ago. They talked about their babies with great candor and emotion. They assured us that they had been as grief stricken and felt as hopeless as we were feeling now. As they spoke, I felt a connection, a tiny ray of hope. "Each baby has a story. Each baby is unique. Each baby has validity." This helped frame all the stories. *Okay, I can get through this night,* I thought.

One by one, each couple spoke of how their babies had died. The mothers did most of the talking, with the fathers nodding in agreement.

As I listened, I had two reactions. First, I had not realized that so many babies died at birth. The parents' stories were eye opening and distressingly sad. I went to the meeting because I did not want to feel so alone, never thinking I would have so much company. My second reaction was more pronounced. All of these babies' deaths were unexpected. These parents did not know in advance, as we had, that their baby would most likely die. That feeling of being different and on our own started to set in.

The meeting was almost over when it was our turn to tell our story. I began but could not finish. "My name is Nancy, and this is my husband, Bryan. Our daughter was born and died this past November, November 17. Her name was Angela." At that point, my courage escaped me and I started to cry. I turned to Bryan, who jumped in and picked up the story. I was so proud of him. He calmly and factually laid out the details of Angela's birth and death. In the meantime, I asked God to help me regain my composure. I was mad at myself; I felt like I was letting Angela down.

One of the group leaders posed a question to me, "What was the hardest part about knowing in advance that your daughter would most likely die?" In response, I explained, "I feel like she died twice. First, when they told us she was going to die, and second, when she actually died in my arms." As I spoke, I felt myself relax, and the warmth of the group seeped over me. Almost universally their responses were akin to the following: "Your story is much worse than mine" or "At least I got to enjoy my pregnancy" or "You never had any good time while you were pregnant." Another woman said, "Your grief started long before your baby was born. You must feel like you've been mourning forever." One of the fathers asked us, "How did you prepare yourself? How did you keep your sanity?"

We learned that one group leader was missing that evening, Cubby LaHood. Her co-leader for the leader said, "Cubby learned early in her second pregnancy that her son had a rare, fatal kidney disorder. Cubby's doctor, who was not very enlightened, told Cubby she should buy a coffin rather than a crib. Cubby has spent the years since her son's death sensitizing doctors and nurses who work in labor and delivery about the care and concern they need to show when a baby dies. I'll make sure Cubby gets in touch with you."

At the end of the session, we were given a prayer card. Taped to the card was a medal on a silver chain. On the card was the following verse from the Old Testament: "See, I will not forget you. I have carved you in the palm of my hand" (Isaiah 49:15). The medal had a rendition of God's hand holding a tiny child. On the back of the card, someone had written, "In loving memory of Angela Mayer-Whittington."

I rode home in silence, clutching my new necklace. Although I had not contributed much, the meeting had helped. Knowing that other mothers out there were facing similar tragedies made my struggle a little easier. I was not glad that other people had lost children; I was just relieved I was not alone. I was encouraged by the prospect of meeting Cubby LaHood. As for my future in MIS, I decided to take it one meeting at a time.

XVII
-MORE THAN A MEMORY -

A few months after Angela's death, I was reading yet another book on bereavement while Molly colored quietly at the breakfast bar. I put down the book in frustration. *Why do these books gloss over the pain? Why do they act as if a child's death is not awful? Was there something wrong with me? Why did it still hurt so much? Why did I still feel so sad?* With each passing week, I felt a little better, with more good days than bad, but I still had this unconscious ache, this nagging feeling. When Molly saw me put down my book, she seized the moment.

"Mommy, did Angela count?" she asked.

I was caught off guard by the question. With Molly, I was always on new ground. I never knew what she might ask me. Following my usual practice, I answered her question with a question of my own.

"What do you mean, 'did Angela count?' "

"Well," said Molly, "Before she was born there were sixteen grandchildren, eight girls and eight boys. Then Angela broke the tie, and we were winning. But then she died. So, did she count?"

I think a lifetime of questions, answers, and frustration went through my head. I had wondered so many of the same things myself: *Angela had lived for only ten minutes. Did that add up to anything? Without Molly and Jessica — living, breathing proof that I was a real mother — would I have been able to call myself a mother? Does ten minutes count? When people ask how many children I have, do I say two or three, or two living and one deceased, or two surviving children? Do I tell people about my daughter in heaven, or is that too much for someone to take in?*

Since I had gone over these questions in my mind a million times, I paused before answering Molly. *I could say that according to the government, Angela counted. We could claim her as a dependent on our income tax that year. But clearly that was a one-time deal and we could never claim her again. I could tell Molly that statements from the insurance company containing Angela's name proved that she counted.* Instead, I just turned to her and said, "Yes, Molly, the girls are winning. Angela counted."

Molly smiled and went back to her coloring. As always, my mind took off. *Did Angela count?* I wanted to shout, *Of course she did!* If Molly, who had lived through the experience and held Angela in her arms, wondered if

Angela counted, how could I expect anyone else to remember her? I drifted back into depression. I knew that my recovery would be a matter of peaks and valleys. Two steps forward and one step back. At that moment I was one step back.

I needed to do something—something big, something to stand the test of time—so that people would remember Angela. Outlandish possibilities converged in my mind. *Should I name a building for her, or maybe a street for her? Should I have a statue erected in her memory, or start a charity in her name?* At this point, I was not quite sure why I needed something big and elaborate as a lasting tribute to Angela. I just knew I was desperately afraid life would go on and the memory of Angela would fade. I needed to do something significant and concrete. I sat up straight while my eyes searched the room for ideas.

My bereavement book slipped off my lap, and as I stooped to pick it up, it hit me. I felt like God, or Angela speaking for God, was talking to me: *Write a book.* The idea rolled around in my mind. *A book—maybe I should write a book.*

One of the things that frustrated me about the books and articles I was reading was the fact that the authors had the advantage of the passage of time to put their thoughts into perspective. Thus, their words lacked the raw pain and overwhelming sadness I was enduring. *Had they, in fact, felt such sorrow? When had their insights occurred?* Two months after Angela's death, I felt stuck. Would I ever have such insights?

Maybe writing about this experience was the answer I had sought. Maybe all that I had experienced with Angela had occurred so I could help other people get through their losses. Maybe the journal entries I had kept so religiously had a long-term purpose. And maybe that purpose was to become the seeds of a book that will tell people like me that in all probability they will experience great pain and cry immeasurable tears as they question the meaning of it all. Without glossing over or diminishing their pain, perhaps I could help them go on. Maybe I could give them some hope, some peace, some tangible ways to deal with their baby's death and find the courage to live again.

I went up to my bedroom and opened my bureau drawer. There, surrounded by souvenirs from my past, was my journal. I opened it to the last entry. I wrote it the day after the funeral. I began re-reading my entries from the beginning. Keeping a journal throughout my pregnancy had been an outlet for me, a safe place to confess my fears and disappointments, reaffirm my confidence in God, and record the events as they unfolded. I did not want to find myself struggling twenty years later with my memory. I sat on my bed and held the journal against my heart. I wanted to pursue this tiny opening in my darkness, this flicker of hope. Maybe the book would be the good that would come from Angela's death. I let the idea take hold. I had longed to be a writer since the fourth grade, but I had settled for a more dependable career. I lacked the courage to pursue writing full time.

Now my mind envisioned a book with the title *Angela* in big, gold letters. Seeming too simple a title, my mind drifted to music coming up the stairs. "What I Did for Love" from *A Chorus Line* was playing, and my mind seized upon *For the Love of Angela*. I rolled it around on my tongue and then spoke it aloud. It had a nice sound.

Since my earliest recollections, I have always felt God's presence in my life. Right then I felt His hand on my shoulder, as if He was saying, *Yes, my child, you are going in the right direction.* The fact that He would accompany me in this long journey was an affirmation of His love. I was not sure what was still ahead of me, but I knew He would be there every step of the way.

XVIII
- BURYING MY DREAM -

When it was time to resume our intimate life, fears which Bryan and I had been harboring since Angela's death came to the surface. He was scared to death we would have another child with Trisomy 18. I was scared to death we would not have another child at all. Indeed, Angela's death hurt more than anything, yet as I sorted through the sadness and pain, I realized that I had not lost my desire to be a mom to another child. Angela's death did nothing to diminish this passion. In fact, it seemed to have fueled it. This desire did not mean anything was lacking in Molly and Jessica. The reality was that I loved them so much that I wanted to have more children just like them. I just knew I had more room in my heart.

For Bryan, Angela's death had the opposite effect. He was so shaken by it that he wanted to make sure it never happened again. At first, I did not understand him. When we talked about it (as we seemed to do all the time initially) Bryan would often say that Angela was the worst thing that had ever happened to him. I came to understand that what he really meant was that losing Angela was the hardest thing he had ever experienced. I wanted him to be able to distinguish Angela, our baby, from the tragic circumstances of her death. After much conversation, Bryan could say that Angela had given us some unbelievable memories, but he did not want to go through it again. He eventually agreed that she was the victim, not the culprit, responsible for all our pain and anguish. As I saw it, she was an innocent participant in our attempts to fulfill our dreams. In truth she was the angel who saved us through the whole experience. Angela was the personification of God's love made visible to us.

Still, despite these concessions, Bryan was adamant that he did not want to conceive another child. Our discussions went something like this:

Me: I know it was awful losing Angela. But, I can't deal with her death and also know I will not have any more children. It is too much.

Bryan: I know how you feel but I'm telling you honestly. I cannot go through the pain of losing another child.

Me: But the doctors have said we are a very low risk for having another Trisomy 18 baby.

Bryan: Can they guarantee that it won't happen again?

Me: You know there are no guarantees.

Bryan: Then, I don't want to risk it.

Me: But don't you see that you are taking away all my hope? My dream of having more children is ending. Can't you understand how hard this is for me?

Bryan: I know how hard it must be. But I'm not changing my mind. Watching Angela die took everything out of me. I can't do it again.

There was no way he could know how I was feeling. There was no way he could know how hard this was for me. How could he? He did not have my hopes and dreams. He did not know that my passion for having a big family consumed me. It was as much a part of me as my heart and soul. My dreams and my conscious thoughts were one and the same.

I waited a month or so and then brought up the subject again. I picked a night when Bryan was in a lighthearted, almost playful mood. I said, "You seem fairly relaxed. Want to try again?" Immediately, his expression changed. His face became guarded and his eyes took on that distant look. He said, "Nancy, our marriage will not survive the uncertainty of trying to have another child."

So, after many tears, sleepless nights, and solitary walks, I too let go of the dream. After each miscarriage I had consoled myself with the knowledge that Bryan and I would try again and, with the help of God, have another baby. Immediately after Angela's death, I clung to the hope that we could and still would have a healthy baby. The desire was both physical and emotional. I needed to hold a baby in my arms, a healthy, breathing baby who needed me as much as I needed him or her. When it became apparent that no amount of crying, pleading, or praying would get Bryan to budge, I gave up. Giving up that hope was almost as hard as giving up Angela.

The desire to have a baby had dominated my thoughts for so long. I always knew I wanted to have children. Long before I was married, I wanted to have a big family. I just knew I was destined to be a mother. Growing up, I would picture myself surrounded by lots of kids. I could see myself taking my family to church, holding the door as my half dozen or so children filed in. Mostly, I took my childhood memories of going to the beach, playing in the backyard, putting together a puzzle, or sitting down to a family meal and imagined myself as my mother basking in the joy of raising a large family. Some people dream of being a rock star; I dreamed about being a mom and having a big family. Giving up that dream was like having a part of me die. Moving on to the next phase of my life was like trying to overcome a tragic defeat.

My life has always been about setting goals and attaining them. I wanted to accomplish a few goals in my professional life before I settled into the role of wife and mother. After high school, I attended the University of Maryland, completing my course of study in four years. I wanted to attend graduate school but did not know which degree to pursue. I thought I would get some work experience first. I began working at the courthouse and, as I worked my way up, decided to pursue a master's degree in Public Administration.

I married Bryan in 1987 and received my graduate degree a year later. Molly was born in 1989. Two years later, I was selected to be the first female Clerk of the District Court for the District of Columbia. I had risen to the pinnacle of my profession by setting goals, using milestones to measure my progress, and then working hard to achieve my objectives. So far no goal had eluded me. With study, hard work, and some divine intervention, I had been able to accomplish everything I set out to do.

Now, I was faced with a goal that I could not achieve by more hard work, education, or persuasive debate. This goal eluded conventional intervention. It defied the usual standards and challenged my soul. Instead of giving birth to several children and triumphantly moving forward to the next stage of raising them, I was on my knees crawling away. I felt cheated, robbed of my childbearing years.

After four months of intense grief over Angela's death, I felt like I was knocked down by this decision not to conceive another child. It was not the same raw pain I felt after Angela died, but it was just as pervasive and numbing. When I could face my situation logically, when the haze of despair and anguish had lifted, I understood that I needed to move on. My age and number of miscarriages were too much to overcome. At first, these moments of lucidity were rare; I mainly felt sorry for myself and spun myself into a cocoon of self-pity. Prayer was my only salvation. I talked with God and asked Him to help me find what I was seeking, to help me look past my immediate situation and look to the future.

My relationship with Bryan suffered as we were tentative and cautious with each other. His relationship with God depended on our situation with Angela; I was more focused on the long haul. He wanted to draw conclusions and move on; I wanted to put everything into perspective. We were in uncharted territory without a map.

In May 1995 Bryan suffered a serious, but non-fatal heart attack. We were caught by surprise, unprepared for the consequences. We thought we were handling Angela's birth and death adequately. We were wrong. With education, time, and family love and support, we discovered we were not as far apart as we had thought. Our common denominator was our love for Molly and Jessica. With God's help, we held on and held together. We did not know what our next steps would be, but we knew we would take them together.

XIX
- Isaiah's Promise -

I faithfully attended the MIS meetings into mid-1995. Bryan's second meeting was also his last; he did not feel like he was getting any benefit from them. I, on the other hand, grew stronger with each meeting. I became good friends with Cubby LaHood, the group leader whose son, Francis Edward, had died from a kidney disorder. After the third meeting, I felt that God was calling me to use my tragedy to support others in their grief.

A year later, at Cubby's urging, I became an MIS group leader. I listened to the stories and offered my support. My counsel generally took the following shape:

Nothing can take away the immeasurable sense of grief and loss you are feeling. Time will help, but in the meantime don't rush back into your former world. Be patient with yourself. Take time with your grief; go through it, not around it. It will be harder now but much better in the long run. Read a lot, talk a lot, pray even more, and listen, just a little, to advice from those who have not experienced your pain. You know yourself best; draw on that strength.

I also learned that grieving is different for everyone. Bryan and I handled our mourning in disparate ways. I was very vocal; he was very quiet. I thought he was not hurting as much because he did not express himself as I did. What works for one person does not necessarily work for another. Bryan and I allowed each other to grieve in our own ways, and this helped us to start the healing process.

After three years of being a group leader for MIS, I needed to change my focus. I was doing a good enough job helping couples cope with the deaths of their children, but I knew I wanted to work more with couples who were facing pregnancies similar to mine. I wanted to make sure that they did not face the nightmare on their own.

Cubby and I talked at length. We both agreed that our pregnancies would have been a little easier if we could have spoken to someone who had gone through a similar experience. We needed someone who could relate to our feelings, answer questions, and support us by listening and being present for the many ups and downs of the pregnancy.

In 1997 Cubby and I began a support group called Isaiah's Promise. We based the name on the same Bible verse used by the MIS group: "See,

I will not forget you. I have carved you in the palm of my hand" (Isaiah 49:15). We developed a brochure stating that we offer "support for parents continuing their pregnancy after a severe or fatal diagnosis," and that we are a group founded by friends in honor of our children.

I never thought when we started Isaiah's Promise that the first couple we would support would be my cousin Mara and her husband, Phil. Mara and Phil were living, temporarily, just outside of London while Phil worked for an international banking firm. They had two wonderful sons, T. J. and Brendan. When they learned that their unborn child was a daughter, Mara and Phil were thrilled, but their joy was fleeting. An early sonogram showed that their daughter had a heart condition which would require surgery immediately after her birth. The surgery was extremely risky and had only been performed successfully in a few hospitals. Fortunately, one of those hospitals was located in London.

So, there Mara and Phil were, away from family and friends and facing the toughest time of their lives. I called Mara and tried to give her a hug across the ocean. I tried to help her sort out her feelings and give her a long-distance shoulder to cry on. But mostly, I tried to listen. Mara was highly perceptive, and her strength constantly amazed me. We talked every two weeks or so, and I sent her reading material and notes of encouragement.

Their daughter, Sara Margaret DeKemper, was born on July 6, 1997. She required forty-eight hours to stabilize before the surgery, which was scheduled in a hospital different from the one in which she had been delivered. Phil rode with Sara in the ambulance, where he told her how brave she was and how much he loved her. He also told Sara that if it was too much for her and she needed to let go and slip off to heaven, he and Mara would understand. Sara passed away peacefully on her way into the operating room. Though heartbroken, Mara and Phil were at peace with the knowledge that Sara was in heaven.

Mara and Phil brought Sara home to bury her and have a memorial Mass celebrated for her. As hard as it was for Mara, she felt she had spent the time before Sara's birth preparing for the fact that Sara would probably not live. My experience had helped Mara, while Mara helped me reaffirm Angela's life. Sara is buried a short distance from Angela, and I have an image of Sara and Angela holding hands, contentedly waiting for us to join them. I sensed that God gave me Angela so I could help Mara celebrate Sara's short life.

Another baby I remember so well is Tikvah Ariella. I met Tikvah's mother, Lisa, over the phone in early April 1998. Lisa and her husband had just received the devastating news that their baby had Trisomy 18. Lisa and I spoke on the phone every two weeks from April until Tikvah's birth in September. Lisa was an Orthodox Jew, but we shared a belief in a compassionate God. That common belief had sustained both of us throughout our lives. Working with Lisa taught me that my Christian roots were not necessarily an impediment to my ability to support someone of another faith. I learned that we both believed in the same God, the God Who supported both of us during our pregnancies with Angela and Tikvah.

Tikvah was born on September 10, 1998. Lisa called me from the hospital, and we were both thrilled that her baby, although very sick, was alive and breathing on her own. I visited Tikvah in the hospital a few days later and could not take my eyes off of her. When Lisa invited me to hold her infant daughter, I was overjoyed. I was able to do something I had never been able to do before and have never had the good fortune to repeat. I picked up Tikvah, and she opened her eyes and looked at me. She even made some baby sounds, and I was mesmerized. I saw what I would have seen in Angela had she lived longer. I knew Tikvah was not Angela, but she was the closest thing to having her back. I wanted those few minutes to go on forever.

With tears streaming down my face, I thanked Lisa for allowing me to share in her time with her daughter. I will never forget that moment and the privilege of holding that little cherub. I sensed that God let me go back in time and relive my precious moments with Angela. He gave me a view of heaven while I was more alert and aware of the miracle.

Tikvah went home from the hospital a few days later. I visited her several times, and I was able to hold her, feed her, and even change her diaper. Each visit was very special, but nothing could replicate my experience of the day of her birth. Sadly, Tikvah died peacefully at home a little over a month after she was born. Lisa and her family thanked me for all that I had done for them, but they had done far more for me. I caught a glimpse of Angela in Tikvah. The glimpse was unanticipated and fleeting, but miraculous. I thanked them, and God, for the gift of Tikvah.

A friend described our work through Isaiah's Promise as "co-suffering." She said Cubby and I are walking with these couples through their sorrow. We cannot take their sorrow away, but we can be there to suffer with them. Maybe that is our vocation.

XX
- MOTHER'S DAY AND BEYOND -

The first year following Angela's death was the hardest. Thanksgiving was awful and Christmas was depressing, to say nothing of my birthday in February. My custom is to take the day of my birthday off to do some fun things just for myself and then celebrate at dinner with Bryan, Molly, and Jessica, when she could be with us. That year I was so sad and lonely I did not want to get out of bed. I knew from my readings that anniversaries and other holidays can trigger strong emotional reactions. I thought, incorrectly, that since my birthday came almost three months after Angela's death, I would be better, but I was not. I was so sad that I vowed to plan upcoming holidays such as St. Patrick's Day, Easter, and Mother's Day. Having a plan helped prevent the demons from sneaking up on me and taking charge of my day. It never completely defeated them, but it did make me feel less defeated.

Mother's Day was bittersweet. Molly made a present for me in school. She was so excited, knowing I would just love it. Her happiness was contagious, and I hung on to it for as long as I could. But I was back on the roller coaster, and it was a long ride.

The Friday before Mother's Day, I attended a memorial Mass for people whose children have died. The Mass was started many years ago to help mothers cope with Mother's Days without the child, or, in some cases, without the children who had preceded them to heaven. It was good being in church, talking to God about Angela at a Mass designed for such remembrances. I cried throughout the service, but it felt safe to cry there. The candles, the music, the rituals of the Mass, and a community brought together to remember their deceased children—all gave me a sense of peace.

Although the Mass was helpful, it was not enough. I wanted more. When I mentioned this to another bereaved parent, she wondered if anything, besides having our children back with us, would be enough. I examined my feelings in this light but still concluded that the Mass was not personal enough. I wanted to hear more prayers referencing children, and, more important, I wanted to hear Angela's name.

As the years passed by, I became better acquainted with the people who organized the Mass. My friend Cubby LaHood was the primary force behind it. She was open to any suggestion that might make the Mass as relevant as possible to the people attending. But even with God's direction, change, like many things, comes slowly.

Seven years later, I had the opportunity to read aloud all the names of the children for whom the Mass was being offered. It was such a satisfying experience that I wondered if this serenity was because I had read Angela's name or because it had been seven years since her death. The integration of Angela's spirit into my soul, the integration I had longed for in the time immediately after her death but had been unable to attain, was finally occurring. I was finding some measure of peace.

Each year on Angela's birthday, our family celebrates her life We follow the same ritual. First, we go to Mass, then to the cemetery. At the cemetery we talk about Angela and read letters and poems. At first Bryan and I took turns reading, and when Molly learned to read, she helped out. We always say three Hail Marys, sing "Happy Birthday," and release a bouquet of balloons to Angela in heaven. I also carefully wipe off Angela's grave marker and place an assortment of fresh flowers on her grave.

For the first few years, many members of our extended family were able to join us. One year, I was too late with my request to have the 9:00 a.m. Mass on November 17 offered for Angela. Blessedly, Father Fangmeyer, who had counseled us throughout my pregnancy and had conducted Angela's graveside service, offered to celebrate a Mass for Angela in our home. No other memory from Angela's anniversaries stands out as vividly. Twenty-five family members gathered in our living room for the liturgy. Father Fangmeyer made it so personal and incorporated everyone into the service. The experience was spiritually satisfying and uplifting.

As the years passed, family attendance at the annual birthday Mass for Angela dwindled out of necessity. My sisters, however, would write me notes and let me know how they had remembered Angela on her special day. One year, my sister Maureen, who lived in California, wrote:

> *We began our preparation for Angela's birthday last week. Leah, Oliver, and Russell like the balloon idea so much they wanted to do something similar. Leah and Oliver each took a note to their teacher on November 17 requesting that their classes join in prayer or song in memory of Angela. They each were given a chance to tell their friends about Angela and how we would celebrate her birthday later that day. They asked their class to join them in prayer. Our note also asked that prayers be said for you and your family and*

all those in faith communities around the world who have experienced or will experience the death of a sweet infant.

That evening, we took our four birthday balloons complete with a treat taped to each one (we choose pixie sticks so the flight would be speedier). Then we said our prayers and released them near the belfry at St. Paschal's into a starry heaven. God bless you all.

From my sister Rosemary:

I will try to make the 9:00 Mass on Angela's special day. I think of all of you often and wonder how you cope with your loss on a daily basis, but most especially at this time of year. Matt, Mark, Kevin, and Kerry are very familiar with Angela's gravesite and the surrounding chimes we ring for her. I love to visit her there and talk to the kids about her life and how her soul is in heaven.

From my sister Mary Pat:

I think of Angela almost every day. I said a special rosary for her and to her on her special day. I don't think you have to worry that she will ever be forgotten. My thoughts of her are very special and peaceful ones. I look back on the day she was born and know that it strengthened my faith more than any other day has. It makes me smile when I think of all of us there and the presence of God in the room. I don't think I could adequately describe it to anyone who was not there. But all of us who were there, I know, felt the same thing.

I keep all the cards, notes, and emails in special boxes devoted to Angela's memory. We had to expand to two boxes to keep up with everything. I hope to have ten boxes one day. It is emotionally satisfying yet bittersweet to know that Angela had an impact on so many people.

God bless Angela.

XXI
- THE JOURNEY CONTINUES -

More than ten years later, life is good. It has been a long journey filled with ups and downs. Just when I thought I was doing well and getting better, I would relapse and find myself sad and crying. There is a saying that when one door closes, another door opens. Although I found the open door shortly after Angela's death, it took some time before I was able to crawl through it.

Now I have the benefit of thirteen hard-won years of that journey. As I reflect upon my pregnancy with Angela and her brief earthly life, I realize how much I have learned about and come to appreciate the dignity and uniqueness of the human person. Angela taught me that about herself— but also about so many others, both in my extended family and in my marriage. For example, I have come to see concretely how men and woman often process information and life experiences differently—and that this is especially true when faced with a situation like Bryan and I faced.

I lived daily with Angela's physical presence within my body. Bryan did not. Thus, because his body was not physically impacted by our daughter's growing presence, he could continue outwardly his regular life. Bryan tended to deal with the situation as it was presented to him while I more often explored endless (frightening) possibilities and "what ifs." I tended to move constantly from my Angela world to my real world while Bryan was much more practical. Although this brought tension to our relationship, it also kept us on a steady course, moving forward. I was often confused by Bryan's ability to move forward while I was so focused on immersing myself in my Angela world. *Why couldn't he stay in the Angela world with me? Did that mean that he cared less for me, for Angela? Did I have to live in my Angela world alone, seeming to bear the pain alone? Why wasn't her dad with me there, in the way that I wanted?*

I came to understand that Bryan dwelt in a world of pain, too—with its differences from mine, yes – but with many similarities. In his world, he still moved out into his professional life each day, oftentimes without the benefit of the sympathetic surroundings that I experienced in my environment. Had Bryan dwelt nonstop in that Angela world with me, no one would have gotten groceries, paid the bills, and kept our daily life moving forward.

We have experienced differences, too, in our spirituality as we have grieved and as we have persevered in our family life. Our faith backgrounds were different and we saw those differences expressed in our grief. Bryan shaped his perspectives about God based upon how things turned out. On the other hand, I shaped my view about how things turned out upon my perspectives about God. Both faith viewpoints have presented challenges and promoted growth for us as individuals and as a couple, but we rest in the knowledge of God's love for us and in our love for one another.

For the Love of Angela is written from my point of view as Angela's mother. If Bryan had written his account, I've come to learn, it would have been far, far different from mine. He was there in support for me, for Angela, for Molly, and for Jessica in every way that he could be—he just reacted differently. I know from my work with MIS groups and the couples we've counseled through Isaiah's Promise that this disparity in reaction is not atypical. When couples experience intrinsic differences in coping and grieving, both mother and father can become hurt and a wedge can develop between them. Some couples never recover. Others, with God's help, learn and grow and work on their recovery. They come to know that they have received gifts disguised as challenges and are far better for having received those gifts.

I've learned anew how expectations and differences can be expressed in the extended families. Some might cringe when they read my recounting of Molly's hospital visit immediately after Angela's death. Others will find quite familiar and reassuring the presence of Molly and fifteen members of my extended family, all who upheld the tradition of being on hand for the birth of each new grandchild. Bryan's family had always chosen differently—preferring to visit newborn Molly when we returned from the hospital. We so took these precedents for granted that we neglected to communicate clearly to Bryan's family that they could be present at Angela's birth. No longer do we assume so much about others' needs and feelings; we have learned so much about love from our dear little Angela and we continue to grow in love because of her.

That growth in love has been expressed in the growth of our family. In 1997 Bryan and I looked into adoption. We briefly explored adopting an infant before learning that in the United States there are more prospective adoptive parents than there are infants to adopt. We were considering an international adoption when a headline in the *Washington Post* caught our attention. President Clinton had just signed a bill making it easier to adopt children through the foster-care system. We spent the evening of our tenth wedding anniversary attending an informational meeting about becoming foster parents.

Almost five years after Angela's death, we welcomed into our lives two young sisters, four-year-old Jordan, and three-year-old Deena. Two years later, in October 2001, they officially became part of our family. Finally, the pervasive feeling that I was destined to have more children, even after all the miscarriages and Angela's death, miraculously came to fruition. Today, Jordan and Deena are beautiful delightful young ladies who have adjusted well to their new family. Along with Molly, they love being aunts to Jessica's children, Nate and Victoria. We are a blended family, a family centered on God, a family deeply blessed.

Had we not been able to adopt, I still would have been complete and fulfilled as the mother of Molly, Jessica, and Angela. Helping Molly and Jessica grow into sensitive, intelligent, spirited, lovely young women has been a major highlight and blessing in my life. Each time I felt like my life was falling apart, with the heartache of my miscarriages and the bitter tragedy of Angela's death, God picked up the pieces and made something beautiful—the happiness of being a stepmother to Jessica, the joy of being Molly's birth mother, and the elation of adopting Jordan and Deena. God is good.

If I had to relive my experience with Angela, I would not really change much. I am not referring to the things over which I had no control, such as Angela's death. I am referring to the decisions I made before, during, and after Angela's arrival. Unlike parents who face the unexpected death of their infant, Bryan and I had a great deal of time to prepare and plan. And plan we did. In retrospect, however, I would have done two things differently. First, I would have taken more pictures. I am not sure what is missing from the pictures we did take; I just know I would have taken more of them. Second, I wish I had a memory of singing to my baby. I know I sang to her before she was born, but not in the ten minutes she was alive. Just one Irish lullaby.

Despite the pain and small regrets, I have some positive and lasting memories. I do still have my Angela moments. They come less frequently, but when they do, they catch me off-guard. Early on, I would generate these moments as my tributes to her and to spend time with her. Now, they come on their own, out of the blue. They surprise me and warm my heart—her soft, fragrant skin; her rich, dark hair; or her clenched but very determined hands. In the beginning, these moments often reduced me to tears, and I had to try desperately to hide them. Now these recollections bring more smiles than tears. These private and powerful memories of Angela erase the world around me and focus my thoughts on her.

During the first year there were, admittedly, few moments when I did not think about Angela. And when I did, I often felt guilty about that. Over time, I realized that instead of dominating my conscious thoughts, she was weaving her way through my subconscious. She was there even when I did not have concrete thoughts about her.

I clearly remember the doctor at my earliest sonogram telling me that Angela was a keeper. She knew my history, yet based on what she was seeing, she thought I would hold on to this baby. When I eventually learned about Angela's condition, the word "keeper" kept haunting me. A keeper is someone who, despite the competition or circumstances, made the cut, survived the culling-out process, and achieved some permanent status. How could Angela possibly have qualified? Yet a keeper she was, not in the sense the doctor intended, but in the eternal sense. Her short life marked my life, and the lives of others, forever. In death she achieved an everlasting life. She was a keeper.

I have always been self-reflective, goal-driven, and results-oriented, but too often I was motivated by fear: the fear of failure, the fear of disappointing someone, the fear of being alone, the fear of not living up to my potential, and my biggest fear, that of losing my child. When my worst nightmare came to pass, it put in perspective all my other fears. Their stranglehold on me was broken. Today I am no longer driven by fear; I am driven by the love of one four-pound, eight-ounce masterpiece. I am driven by the overwhelming feeling that I did the right thing: I gave Angela the only life I could give her. I did it out of love for her.

I have learned that life, sometimes, is about death. It is about learning to go on and remembering what has been lost. I survived Angela's death by going through the experience, not around it or over it. I crawled through it at first, then slowly found my bearings and started to walk. But instead of trying to go on and forget, I went on and remembered. I took Angela with me, and I am so much better for having her life permanently entwined with mine.

I do not yet have all the answers to my questions of why Angela had to die, why I was chosen to carry her, and how I can better integrate her into my life. What I am learning, though, is not exactly what I thought I would learn. Angela's life and death showed me clearly that life can be lived fully and completely in the space of a few minutes. As Christians, we spend all of our time on earth living a life that is deserving of a final reward, heaven. Some people attain that final reward after many years of upright living. Some attain it after many hard years of searching. Some never look, never search, never prepare, and some are chosen by God to epitomize Edgar A. Guest's verse: "'I will lend you, for a little tme, a child of mine,' God said." Angela showed me that every life has value, purpose, and meaning.

What does the future hold? I intend to raise my daughters to leave a legacy of strong faith, good works, and unconditional love. Is everything perfect? No way. I still have my dark times and dark days, but I manage to live every day with the feeling that through Angela, my eyes, heart, and soul are better attuned to finding ways to help others. Because of Angela, I find ways to honor her life while inspiring others to learn, grow, and find peace in their children's life and death.

Life, then, is a journey from birth to death, with the goal of leaving the world a slightly better place. As Mother Teresa said, "We can do no great things, only small things with great love."

Small things, done in Angela's name, with great love, have been and are my legacy.

And so, the journey continues.

GOD HAD A PLAN FOR THE FAMILY

It's Mother's Day,
I'm just mowing the lawn,
Those thoughts of you
Keep coming on,
I see your eyes,
I see your face
Wanna touch your skin,
God's gentle grace
A bit of heaven
Came down to us,
Though you weren't here long,
Your love touched our hearts.

Refrain:
Oh, tiny cherub
Sent from above,
You gave us strength,
We gave you love.
A happy life that wouldn't be,
God had a plan for the family.
The days without you
No longer grind,
What Daddy wouldn't give
To hold you—just one more time.

The doctor said
That you wouldn't live long,
Incompatible with life—
With all that was wrong.
We made the choice to carry on,
Give you a chance,
We'd all be strong.
The months went by,
We felt you grow
Kept safe inside,
You wouldn't let go.
Molly was right,
She couldn't wait,
Just holding you,
That would be so great.

Refrain

We spent your life in a sterile place,
The whole family came
To see your face.
They all stayed, many hours spent,
Just holding you, a lifetime's rent.
We have you now in photographs
You are in our hearts,
We sometimes laugh,
Imagine you at six years old
Mommy's parents are there
For you to hold.

Refrain

It's still Mother's Day,
Everything's all right,
Few minutes more
'Til we visit the sight,
A little bronze plaque
Now marks the spot,
Left here on earth,
Although you're not,
Hear sounds of wind chimes
In the trees,
Love's message sent
Upon the breeze.
Reach down from heaven
And hold our hands
Though we can't feel you,
It helps us pretend

Refrain, then repeat:
What Daddy wouldn't give to hold
you just one more time.

by Bryan Richard Whittington

ACKNOWLEDGMENTS

Writing this book was the antidote that God provided to help me heal and share Angela's story. Over time, I had a series of insights and God helped me to connect the dots. Thank you, dear God, for being so good to me!

There are so many other people who have helped me with this book and who have celebrated Angela's life. My thanks and unconditional love go to my husband Bryan whose love for Angela and whose support of my writing mean more to me than I can ever express. To my daughter Molly, your presence in my life is my greatest joy. To Jordan and Deena, loving both of you has made me the happiest mother in the world. And, Jessica, my love for you, Jason, Nate, and Tori is boundless. Thank you, my family, for integrating Angela into your lives and honoring her memory in all that you do.

To my sisters and their families: Mary Pat and Tom George, Kathleen and John Bovello, Celeste and Chuck Kerner, Susie and Don Van Gieson, Eileen and Jeff Pryor, Maureen and Otis Sangster, Rosemary and Richard Stein, Liz and George Welton, and Cecilia and Tony Rowedder, your faith in God, your commitment to your family, your service to others, and your love that knows no limit have enriched and inspired me more than you will ever know.

To the Whittington family, especially Nina and Paul, Rosalie, Michelle and Diane, thank you for all your love.

To my good friend, Cubby LaHood, I cannot thank you enough for leading me through my recovery and helping me to channel my grief into something positive and satisfying. You and your husband Dan, as lay Missionaries of Charity, are truly doing God's work on earth.

Thank you to Dr. Paul McCauley for reviewing my very rough manuscript and making sure my representations were medically accurate, and even more importantly, for encouraging me and supporting my efforts to publish this book. Thank you, Dr. McCauley, for writing such a beautiful endorsement.

Thanks to Father Lee Fangmeyer: your prayers, support, and kindness to our family will never be forgotten.

Thank you also to my publishers, Father Daniel Mahan and Jean Zander. Your enthusiasm and appreciation of Angela's story are gifts unto themselves. Your hard work and willingness to publish my book are blessings that I never thought I would realize. God bless both of you!

My deep appreciation goes to Mary Beth Newkumet whose encouragement to pursue publishing resulted in her connecting me with Saint Catherine of Siena Press. Thanks to Rochelle Melander who twice edited my book and made it a much better work because of her insightful suggestions.

Chief Judge Thomas F. Hogan of the United States District Court for the District of Columbia, thank you for inspiring me through your life's work and for always supporting me in my vocations. To Judge John Garret Penn, thank you for being such a wonderful influence in my life. To Magistrate Judge John Facciola and Circuit Judge David Sentelle, your endorsement of Angela's life is much appreciated.

LeeAnn Hall, you are the best friend anyone could ever have. You've accompanied me on so many of my life's journeys, I don't know what I would do without you. Denise Curtis and Debbie Jason, my good friends who encourage me and support me always, thank you for all that love.

Finally, a special thanks to my courthouse family for making my life so much richer by your kindness and friendship. To my assistant, Peggy Trainum, thank you for organizing my early efforts after hours and on your own. Bridget Kerner, your photography is incredible! And to my sister, Kathleen Bovello, thank you for all the support and love. I would not have gotten this book published without you.

A graduate of the University of Maryland and The George Washington University, author Nancy Mayer-Whittington is the Clerk of the Court, United States District Court for the District of Columbia. She is the cofounder of Isaiah's Promise, a support group for parents continuing a pregnancy after a severe or fatal diagnosis. Nancy and her husband, Bryan, have five children and two grandchildren. *For the Love of Angela* is her first book.
